D1555247

SYSTEMS OF ORGANIZATION

SYSTEMS OF ORGANIZATION

Management of the Human Resource

David G. Bowers

Ann Arbor
The University of Michigan Press

First edition as a paperback 1977
Copyright © by The University of Michigan 1976
All rights reserved
ISBN 0-472-08172-1 (clothbound)
ISBN 0-472-08173-X (paperbound)
Library of Congress Catalog Card No. 75-31052
Published in the United States of America by
The University of Michigan Press and simultaneously
in Rexdale, Canada, by John Wiley & Sons Canada, Limited
Manufactured in the United States of America

Preface

This is a book by one man about the ideas of another. As such, it is an attempt by the former to rephrase in his own words the concepts and contributions of the latter. The author has attempted to present not his own ideas—for even in close collaboration over a period of time creative differences persist—but to present the views and ideas of the scholar himself.

In the course of writing this book, the author has been struck by several impressions which justify being shared. One is the continuity of the ideas of Rensis Likert over the length of his professional career. Few "dead ends" appear; ideas instead appear to have evolved over the years, being shaped and developed as new research findings and insights fill voids which could only be handled with difficulty at an earlier date. Another is the foresightedness in relation both to events and to concepts: in some instances ideas subsequently presented and elaborated independently by others at a later date appear much earlier, in clearly recognizable form, in the writings of Rensis Likert. In at least a few instances he has given a brief glimpse of the future in terms which bear an uncanny resemblance to the subsequent stream of actual events.

What is presented in this book is much condensed; the interested reader may turn to the original material for greater elaboration. Perhaps most importantly, what is presented is prologue, because Rensis Likert continues to research, refine, integrate, and publish his ideas.

David G. Bowers

Contents

CHAPTER 1

Prologue

For a number of years, Rensis Likert has been respected as one of the leading thinkers and writers in the organizational management area. For some, theory is spun in an armchair, from the informal observations of a creative mind, but with little systematic evidence as its base. Likert's ideas and concepts are, however, only speculative to the extent that theory attempts to develop a plausible explanation of existing findings. They have been based instead upon research. His theory of management systems, organized and stated in an integrated fashion in *New Patterns of Management*[1] and *The Human Organization*,[2] has been derived from a vast quantity of concrete evidence, obtained from looking, measuring, weighing, and analyzing actual events in real organizations.

Although his initial ideas and views in this area appear in publications authored while he held earlier positions in academic, business, and government life, it has been in the twenty-five years from 1946 to 1971, at the Institute for Social Research, that his efforts, findings, and concepts have attained that critical mass necessary for classification as a formal theory. He has cited and drawn upon the work of his colleagues, as they have drawn upon his, and the organizational public is the richer for it.

The strategy he has followed in building his concepts into a theory is simple, straightforward, and readily understood: he and his colleagues have gone out into the real world and looked in a systematic way at what members of organizations, and organizations themselves, do. By comparing what those organizations and subunits which are highly effective do differently from those which are less effective, they have put together a picture of a way of management that rather consistently produces better operating and human results. Whereas early studies selected, for example, twenty highly effective and twenty ineffective sales offices or service units and looked at differences in management practices between the two clusters, later studies have looked more closely at highly specific criteria of performance, such as sales volume per unit, cost performance, grievance rate, accident rate, and the like. Although elaborated over the years, as simple concepts turned out to be much more complex, the findings have been consistent: American managers who do the best job of managing employ different, and more sophisticated, methods and principles of handling the human organization than do those whose record is less successful.

These practices and principles can be elaborated in considerable detail, and they will be presented in at least adequate form in subsequent chapters. In overview terms, however, they may be summarized very simply. They consist of concepts of what an organization is, and what it is not. An organization is not simply a physical plant or its equipment. It is not an array of positions, nor a collection of persons who fill those positions. It is not a sequence of work tasks or technical operations. It is all of these things, to be sure, but it is fundamentally something more. The basic building block of the organization is the face-to-face group, consisting of the supervisor and those subordinates immediately responsible to him. The organization consists most basically of a structure of groups, linked together by overlapping memberships into a pyramid through which the work flows.

All groups are essential; all are characterized by the same basic processes that make them function either well or poorly. By the scope of their authority and responsibility, however, groups nearer the top of the pyramid have a greater effect upon the conditions within which groups nearer its base must work than the latter have upon the former. The productive output of top management groups, for example, consists of procedures, objectives, and policies which profoundly affect the lives of groups at lower ranks and their ability to do their jobs.

Within any group, a sequence is set in motion by the behavior of the group's supervisor. His actions toward his subordinates set the tone for their behavior toward one another and for their performance on the job. An effective supervisor accomplishes through his behavior the building of a group oriented toward cooperative accomplishment of the task or mission. In contrast, an ineffective supervisor sets in motion through his actions patterns of behavior which detract from, or depress, that performance.

These connections, between the behavior of supervisor and subordinates within groups and among groups linked by supervisors to one another, gravitate the organization gradually toward a "system" of management—a pattern of practices, behaviors, and beliefs that is internally consistent and distinguishable from other such systems. One management system may be harsh, autocratic, reluctant to act at all from fear of acting improperly, unwilling to share information internally, and possessing little real ability to maintain anything resembling real control over events which affect it. Another system may be characterized by feelings of great motivation and loyalty, a sense of involvement and commitment to the organization and its objectives, and a willingness to pool all information and available know-how in an effort to make certain that all goes well. Research findings indicate rather conclusively that organizational effectiveness—good performance in the operating records as well as in the human spheres of satisfaction and well-being—is primarily the result of the management system in use in the organization, not its cause, nor merely its companion.

That system which appears to function best in American industry is participative, in the sense that it encourages an open sharing of information and the involved influence by members over events and decisions affecting their lives. It is also group based; it makes use of cooperative work teams at all levels, rather than relying upon the man-to-man pattern of relationships most common in less effective systems.

Consistent with these findings are certain assumptions and principles about the nature of man and his desires. There is a belief, strongly held by many theorists and recognized in practice by many of the most effective managers, that each person wants appreciation, recognition, influence, a feeling of accomplishment, and a feeling that people who are important to him believe in him and respect him. Each person wants to feel that he has a place in the world. This desire appears to be universal and seems to be the basis for some of the general principles used by the most effective managers.

Against a backdrop of this need for a sense of personal worth and importance, the behavior of an individual within the limits of a given situation stems from his skills, his concept of what he is supposed to do (his cognitive orientation), and his will to do it (his motivation). A management system which denies him influence, appreciation, respect, and confidence diminishes his motivation to be a contributing member of the organization; a management system which provides those positive conditions enhances it.

Autocracy, whether in industry, government, or society at large, is run on fear. It requires compliance with directives, adherence to edicts of the few in powerful positions. As such, it suppresses separate ego recognition for the great mass of individual members. There may be, to be sure, some vicarious feeling of recognition by persons in the rank and file membership through identification with a particularly charismatic leader. This rapidly wears thin, however, leaving a punitive base as the principal source of motivation available to most members.

It is for this reason that autocratic management carries as its by-product a certain emotional immaturity. Fear leads to intellectual malfunctioning, which leads to ineffective response. Emotional maturity means, in part, well-established habits of tackling problems with the brain in full control of the emotions, a condition not particularly enhanced by fear of punishment.

The autocratic organization, therefore, faces the world at a serious disadvantage. Not only does it lack that enthusiasm for accomplishing the mission or objective that we call motivation, it creates for itself the illusion of power and control, an illusion based on the obvious absence of overt resistance. It usually accrues to itself a fund of resentment just under the surface, a feeling of some pleasure on the part of subordinate members at the prospect of management's falling on its face (if not a willingness to help that process along). But perhaps more damaging than any of these, it creates an inability to solve problems and make decisions optimally, partly because fear paralyzes, even in the management ranks, and partly because it systematically denies to itself access to information available in the lower echelon of the organization.

If this has always been inherent in the autocratic organization, the problem which it creates for organizational management waxes more critical in present days than it did earlier. There was perhaps a time, when a large number of jobs were unskilled, when technology was relatively uncomplicated, and when an individual's economic security was more tenuous, in which acquiescence to autocratic directives was more easily obtained and the impact of negative motivational consequences upon the organization's outcomes smaller than it is now. Not only are changes in these conditions rapidly accelerating, such that a large number of operations in most work organizations require the active pooling of information and cooperation from many persons as well as a high degree of technical skill, but societal values are changing as well. Both educational and child-rearing practices are adding to the work force each year numbers of employees accustomed to greater freedom and a larger say over events that affect them. More often than ever before, direct, unexplained orders are flatly rejected and responded to with a suggestion from the employee that the issuer dispatch himself to a warmer climate, a situation which the more autocratic foreman can ordinarily cope with only by disciplinary action which runs the risk of a wildcat walkout. Societal changes have therefore added, to the always present desire for more considerate treatment, greater expectations among employees about how they should be treated, and this has been accompanied by a more secure base from which to make their desires and expectations felt. It is for all these reasons, finally, that organizations whose top officials opt for the pleasant narcosis of autocratic management do so at considerable risk.

In the chapters which follow we shall discuss in some detail those organizational processes, supervisory practices, group relationships, and development procedures associated with greater operating effectiveness of the human organization. In doing so, we shall contrast this more productive system with that autocratic system which we have already described in general terms.

CHAPTER 2

The Central Role of the Work Group

> *Management will make full use of the potential capacities of its human resources only when each person in an organization is a member of one or more effectively functioning work groups that have a high degree of group loyalty, effective skills of interaction, and high performance goals.*[1]

We grow up in groups, and we live in them all our lives. We are born into the family, and we later extend our memberships to include childhood playmate groups, adolescent school groups, postadolescent collegiate and young adult groups, clubs, church groups, and literally dozens of other groups which we join and participate in during a lifetime. In a literal sense, we are brought into this world by a group, to live in a group, and we are carried out of it by a group.

As adult members of society, however, probably no

groups have greater influence upon our lives than a central three: (*a*) our family, (*b*) our work groups, and (*c*) our group of closest friends. The first two are undoubtedly far more important in shaping our lives than the third, if for no other reason than that we spend approximately one-third of our adult lives interacting in the family setting, one-fourth in the work group, and only perhaps one-tenth in recreation or interaction with our closest friends.

It is reasonably accurate, therefore, to say that groups are present everywhere and that, given any large collection of persons, groups of some sort will inevitably form. This does not mean, of course, that all groups are highly effective or are committed to desirable goals. Groups can vary in their effectiveness from poor to excellent; their values and goals can be highly constructive, both for themselves and for the larger organization or society of which they are a part, or they can be highly destructive. They can accomplish a great deal of good, or they can do considerable harm. There is nothing inherently good or bad, contributive or noncontributive, about a group.

Although the group can in this fashion be shown to be a powerful force in all walks of life and in all organizational settings, business or industrial firms have all too often neglected it in their activities and their plans. They usually hire individuals, engineer or design individual tasks, pay individuals as such, transfer or lay off individuals, and promote solely on individual merit. It certainly ought not be suggested that the individual's identity, recognition, and total rewards should be submerged into a collectivity called "the group." It does indicate, however, that work organizations often ignore the fact that the person who succeeds or fails in his tasks, who is hired or laid off, transferred or promoted, is a member of a group, and that the sum total of his reaction to events is highly influenced by that fact. The view that each person should remain at his work station, focused upon his assignment and no other, with a minimum of water cooler traffic, accepting directives issued to him, is naive to say the least.

Some Basic Properties of Groups

The supervisor of a work group exerts a major influence in setting the tone or atmosphere of that work group by his leadership practices and principles, evidenced to the members by his behavior toward them. For this reason, if a group is to be highly effective, the leader must be selected carefully. His leadership ability is so evident that, were the situation an unstructured one, he would probably emerge as the leader.

That the organization must select and appoint supervisors on the basis of their real leadership skill and ability is evidenced by a brief consideration of what the organization can, in fact, give to whomever it appoints to a position. The organization gives a supervisory appointee not a great deal at all, a condition which may come as a shock both to superiors and their subordinate appointees. It gives him some amount of authority (the *right*, but not necessarily the ability, to determine outcomes), and it gives him some real ability to reward and punish (a quantum increasingly constricted or curtailed in recent years, as social legislation and employee organization have become more potent forces). It remains for the appointee himself, however, to develop his real ability in depth to influence outcomes in constructive directions by his expertise and the respect it produces, by group members' liking for him as a person, and *by the kind of group he builds*. If he is unable to build an effective group and is thereby unable really to exercise the supervisory leadership that is required for effective operation, it is likely that an informal leader will emerge who does. If the formal leader is harsh and punitive, relying excessively upon coercion and authority, it is likely that the group will develop solidarity around the informal leader in ways and with aims contrary to the interests and objectives of the larger organization.

In contrast to this, to the extent that the group is positive, rewarding, reassuring, and stimulating, it will be attractive to its members. They will develop a closeness, cohesiveness, confidence, and trust that will result in pride in their group and loyalty to its aims and objectives. The basic motives of persons change little, but the ways in which they satisfy these motives can and do change. Values and expectations change gradually as experience changes, and they shift with changing group memberships. More specifically, we acquire our values and expectations from the face-to-face groups of which we are or have been members. Under the highly effective group conditions just described, therefore, values that seem important to the group will carry a greater likelihood of acceptance by individual members, who will be more highly motivated, not only to abide by those values, but to achieve the important goals of the group.

With these conditions we assume, of course, that the group has been in existence for a sufficient period of time to have developed a well-established, easy working relationship among all of its members. Irrespective of the level of interpersonal sensitivities and group skills present at the outset among its members, each group must develop over time the confidence and trust, loyalty, and motivations which characterize a highly effective group. Members must come to know each other well enough to understand what is meant by information transmitted to them by others. They must know what others mean by their casual remarks and by their behavior in day-to-day situations. Each person must learn his own particular role and the ways in which it relates to the roles of all others in the group. There must be established common expectations and norms of behavior. There appears to be no fully acceptable substitute for time together for developing these close bonds. This fact is often overlooked, even by firms that otherwise take great stock in, and are relatively sophisticated concerning, the use of groups.

Many firms ignore these facts in their rotation policies, for example. Rotation through various assignments, however valuable for development purposes or for meeting immediate needs which stem from fluctuations in manning requirements or markets, tends to prevent work groups from developing those close ties associated with high effectiveness. For this reason, rapid changes in personnel assignments should be avoided as much as possible. The effects of those changes which are absolutely necessary can, of course, be lessened by training all members in group skills, in interpersonal sensitivity, and in the different roles to be performed.

Relationships within Highly Effective Groups

Where members have the interaction skills required for successful performance of all of the various leadership and membership roles, the group's communication, problem-solving, and decision-making activities tend to occur in an atmosphere that enhances members' sense of their contribution, worth, and importance. There is in such a situation a strong motivation on the part of each member to communicate fully and frankly to the group all of the information which is potentially worthwhile to the group's attaining its objectives. There is correspondingly little motivation for members to withhold information, either from fear of ridicule, or because it may be politically expedient to communicate selectively to those other members, including the leader, whom some members wish to influence unilaterally to their own advantage.

Just as there is high motivation to communicate, there is also a strong interest in receiving communications. Knowing each other's needs, interests, and views on most issues, as well as the mutual trust which openness generates, means that less energy is spent by each member in defending in advance against possible "one-upmanships" of distorted representation of viewpoints. Less energy is also spent in attempting to recall which information one has shared with which other members, in attempting to keep one's personal stories "straight." Anyone who has lived for any length of time in an organization run on a mistrust model will recognize the truth of the statement that nothing is so damaging to one's position in such a situation as the discovery that he has given another member the "wrong fraction" of information, or that two members to whom he has communicated selectively half of a whole story have put their halves together and discovered the truth. Autocratic organizations, operated on a man-to-man model, are rife with this type of mental bureaucracy, and they invest a great deal of what might otherwise be productive energy in it. Organizations operated upon a participative-group model, on the other hand, avoid this costly outlay.

The processes of the highly effective group enable the members to exert more influence upon the leader and to communicate far more information to him than is possible in less effective, man-to-man relationships. There are similar strong motivations to try to influence, as well as communicate with, other members, and to be receptive to influence by them. Each member tends to accept willingly, and more nearly without resentment, the goals and expectations that he and the other members establish for the group. Because of these processes, the values and goals of the group are more likely to represent a satisfactory integration of members' values and needs. To the extent that the leader (and in some instances other members as well) are candid about the requirements and needs they feel from other memberships in the organization, they are more likely to be able to bring the present group's goals into line with those larger requirements. There is, therefore, a high motivation in the group to use the communication process in ways which best serve the interests and objectives of both the group and the larger organization.

In the highly effective group, individual members feel secure in making decisions which seem appropriate to them because the goals and operating philosophy are clearly understood by each member and provide him with a solid base for his decisions. When necessary or advisable, other members of the group will give a member the help he needs to accomplish successfully his share of the established goals. There is, under these conditions, less reluctance to set goals that are high, but still reasonable, since the individual knows that help will be forthcoming from his fellows if really needed. In practice, this is manifested by both the leader and the members believing that each group member can accomplish "the impossible," and the group is eager to help each member develop his full potential as a contributing human being.

The reassuring, accomplishment-oriented atmosphere of the highly effective group also stimulates creativity by members. At first, this may appear contrary to fact because it contradicts the commonly accepted belief that strong group identification breeds a petty conformity. In fact, the reverse appears to be true. Freed from the constraints of rivalries, petty jealousies, and the need to "play one's cards close to one's chest," individual members feel more at liberty to explore publicly, alone, and in collaboration with others in the group, new and perhaps unorthodox possibilities. In this way, as in the help provided to one another in times of rush or crisis, the ability of group members to influence one another contributes to the flexibility and adaptability of the group.

Groups are, therefore, a fact of an organization's life, a force the organization can ignore at some considerable risk, or a resource that can naturally accrue to its benefit. The most productive management system presently in use makes use of this resource. For those who adhere to this system, the group is truly the basic building block of the organization.

CHAPTER 3

Participative
Decision Making

The previous chapter discussed at some length the fact that groups which are carefully built and effectively led develop a strong commitment to fulfill the goals which they set for themselves. The statement was made that managers who desire to head highly productive organizations rely upon groups of this kind as fundamental building blocks of their enterprise. The reader with a healthy skepticism will have already asked himself what basis exists for believing that the goals that these groups set for themselves bear any resemblance to those objectives which the organization must have them fulfill for its greater good. Answering this question requires that we look briefly at alternative existing practices.

Likert has described classical management theory as relying ". . . primarily on the economic motives of buying a man's time and then telling him precisely what to do, how to

do it, and at what level to produce."[1] Writing a few years
earlier, he quotes a then current textbook in the management
area as stating that, "The relationship of employer and employee in an enterprise is a contractual obligation entailing
the right to command and the duty to obey."[2] It is one of
the anomalies of our time that research shows that it is in the
low-producing organization, far more often than in the high,
that these injunctions are most closely followed. It is where
performance is less stellar that managers and supervisors tend
to concentrate on keeping their subordinates busily engaged
in going through a specified work cycle in a prescribed way
and at a satisfactory rate as determined by company standards.

The notion that there is one best method of handling
any issue, or of doing any job, suitable for the average person
contains much that is dangerously oversimplified. Except in
rare instances, that average person is nonexistent, which
means that any method so engineered for application to a
large number of persons will be in some measure inefficient,
wrong, uncomfortable, and awkward for nearly all of them.

It would, of course, be much better if the job were separately tailored to fit each person performing it, with his involvement and with a meeting of his needs and capabilities.
Needless to say, this is not ordinarily possible. Interchange-
ability of parts and operations means that at least some standardization is necessary. Schedules and interdependency of
operations means that the work pace is not entirely an open
matter. The need for equitable treatment means that some
rules applicable to all must necessarily be drawn up and en-
forced.

The point, however, is that organizations have all too often gone overboard on matters of standardization, "best"
methods, and sameness. Part of the reason for this is that
there exists a strong scientific management tradition which
has had a tenacious grasp—for good and for ill—upon most of

industry. The stating of this fact should not be taken as indicating a wholesale rejection of that tradition. There are basic, powerful concepts of scientific management that have revolutionized industry and made it much more productive than it otherwise could ever have been:

1. the elimination of waste and inefficiency through functionalization, work simplification, and related processes;
2. the establishment of specific work goals;
3. measurement of work accomplished and the continued examination of the extent to which specified goals are met;
4. coordinated and clear-cut channels of communication, control, and decision making.

The fundamental problem with traditional theories of management is the theory of motivation upon which they are based. They assume a simple, economic man and ignore other powerful motives. Often the result is that practices intended to motivate instead evoke resentments, hostilities, and adverse reactions. The assigned right to control is assumed to be the same as the real power to influence, and costly exceptions—the purposely dented product, the wrench thrown into the conveyor mechanism, the wildcat strike—are treated simply as reflections of the perverseness of human nature. In point of fact, however, they have engineered a certain number of grievances, strikes, and destructive acts into the system, along with the number of product units per hour.

Another related reason for the excessive emphasis upon directed sameness is the management philosophy held by those in many positions of influence in the organization. It is a pessimistic, sour outlook on the work world which holds that men are untrustworthy, basically lazy, and will take as much as they can and give as little as they can get away with. An ugly stepson of the theory of economic man, it concludes that only by rigid routing and constant surveillance will the job be done properly.

This view ignores several basic facts brought to the surface by a great deal of research in recent years. One of these facts is that there exists a well-nigh universal need to feel that one is a contributing member of some entity larger than oneself, to accomplish something meaningful, to do a good job, and to be recognized for it. The same worker who may appear to be lazy on the job will often go home and spend hours laboring over a "do-it-yourself" project for one of his neighbors. The difference, of course, is that this latter activity is one in which he himself is involved and probably consulted, with few artificial status distinctions and with a healthy camaraderie to sustain both the energy and the know-how.

What classical theories overlook, to their motivational detriment, is that there is ordinarily more than one route to meeting an objective, and that some of the routes, equally effective in getting the job done, go a greater distance toward meeting the needs of the persons performing the job than do other routes. When organizations permit those who must do the job to settle on a way of doing it that meets their personal needs, motivational forces felt by employees, many of them ignored by economic man theory, now align themselves in ways which help build a drive toward meeting the organizational objective. They no longer fight progress toward that accomplishment; they instead reinforce it.

Top management persons often comment sarcastically, in talking about participative decision making, that it amounts to "giving the plant away." This view overlooks the fact that most organizational members do not require for their self-fulfillment a personal role in setting basic corporate direction or destiny. They do feel a need, however, and they do appreciate, having a voice in deciding those issues closely related to their own work lives.

However, the anxious executive, interested in maximizing the motivation that comes with involvement, but worried that things may in some way get out of hand, should realize that several built-in restraints normally operate. First, the fact that we live in a relatively open society, in which individuals have considerable freedom of choice and movement with regard to employment, means that selection processes, both self-selection and the formal mechanisms employed by the company, will have produced a degree of gravitation toward the organization in those interested in its objectives and tasks. For example, a relatively introverted man whose primary concerns are for economic security, steady employment within normal hours, without travel, and with a paycheck of known size each week will seldom apply to, let alone be hired by, an organization whose purpose is statewide store-to-store wholesale sales on commission. Therefore, some fitting of member needs to organizational objectives occurs naturally.

Added to this must be the observations made earlie that, although motives remain relatively stable, the means c satisfying them change frequently, with attachments to part cular paths heavily influenced by membership in effectiv groups. In addition, the supervisor sets the tone for the grou by his own behavior, an influence that goes some substanti measure toward generating congruity between the group goals and the organization's objectives.

Finally, some congruity occurs simply because organiz tions are seldom entirely brand new. By the time the broz mass of organizational members arrive on the scene, certain basic situational requirements are already in place. Other sub-units of a parent organization, for example, may depend upon the output of this organization, a fact which sets expectations which members ordinarily can understand and appreciate, if the information is shared with them. Beyond this, certain things are simply not possible in the particular physical and social environment of the organization. Members can comprehend and accept these facts of life, if given the opportunity to do so.

How Participation Works

The elements of participation are simple to list, but more complicated to put into operation. They consist of (*a*) group, rather than man-to-man, methods of supervision, (*b*) the open flow of information in all directions (with immunity from ridicule or vindictiveness), and (*c*) the ability of all parties to exercise a measure of influence over outcomes. A supervisor attempting to follow a participative pattern typically presents to his group in a regular staff meeting a problem which faces them collectively, and *before* any decision has been made about it, encourages all views, makes his own available without presenting it in such a way as to override others, and develops those processes which result in the pooling of all relevant information. From this he helps the group to develop an integrative solution to the problem at hand, one to which they are all, including himself, willing to commit themselves.

As a general rule, at each level the problems considered should be those for which the supervisor of the group has responsibility. For example, if he happens to be the department superintendent, the problems should be those of the department, and not those of the sections whose heads report to him. The problems of the subordinate section head are the appropriate topics for the group of which the subordinate is supervisor. A group can, of course, appropriately address itself to the problems of a subordinate member of the group when that member himself seeks the advice or help of his peers and superior.

In making decisions in this participative group fashion, there are facts, such as deadlines, minimum financial conditions as to earnings or reserves, or the like, which cannot be ignored if the organization is to achieve its objectives. It is the task of the supervisor to be fully aware of these *situational requirements*, and to make his subordinate group aware of them as well. In making decisions, he and his group should never lose sight of them.

If his group is so divided in opinion that it seems unable to reach a consensus decision in the time available, the superior has the responsibility for making a decision which does in fact meet the situational requirements. When this happens, the supervisor may be well advised to accept the solution preferred by the persons who will have the major responsibility for implementing the decision, provided, of course, the supervisor himself feels that the solution is reasonably sound.

Sometimes the differences of opinion are not among members of the work group, but between the supervisor on the one hand and his subordinates on the other. In this event, the superior should present clearly the evidence which convinces him of the point of view he holds. If, after additional discussion, the group still differs with his view, the supervisor faces a difficult decision. He can overrule the group and take the action he prefers, or he can go along with the group and accept the consequences. If the costs of a mistake are likely to be excessive, the supervisor may well feel that he has no choice but to do what his own experience suggests is best. But whatever he elects to do, he is responsible and must accept full responsibility for what follows.[3]

One often hears, especially at the top executive levels of an organization, an expression that indicates that the particular individual who acts in a supervisory capacity believes that he had been chosen for his position because he literally knows more about operations than all others, and that therefore it is his job, and his alone, to make the decisions. In today's increasingly complex organizations and their technologies, however, he is unfortunately likely in fact to be more poorly informed about most operating matters than some of his subordinates. Their knowledge, appropriately extracted and pooled, is likely to outweigh by far in both comprehensiveness and quality anything his own mind could generate. (At least this would be true in a majority of cases.) His responsibility is not to make the best decisions, but to so structure and guide events that the *best possible decisions are made.* This is a fundamentally different task from the one that many executives feel has been cut out for them. Their major concern should be their skill in getting the appropriate, knowledgeable parties together in a process likely to be productive, not their prerogatives or image as personal decision makers.

When he elects, however, to make the decisions himself, he will almost certainly make them on the basis of limited information from one or two subordinates. The fact that others, not necessarily considered relevant to the decision process but necessary for executing it, were not involved, will likely result in foot-dragging by them in a number of critical instances. In addition, subordinates will not share information with one another, but will instead time the sharing of it with him so as to reap a maximum of personal gain. More "yessing" will occur: much of the information he receives will be simply a funneling back to him of what they sense he wishes to hear. The concerns of the whole company (or department, if that is what he heads) will not be the basis for action, but rather the parochial interests of their subunits.

A particularly mistaken impression that often occurs, especially among senior executives who attempt a partial application of participative group decision making, is that groups should be convened by them to discuss issues within one or another of the subordinate departments. On such occasions there is a perception frequently that only certain subordinates should be convened, since the issues of the moment are of concern "only to some." Group processes and group problem solving are as applicable and relevant at this level as at other levels. The top executive who views the situation in this manner is, in the first place, usually dealing with the wrong issues: the problems under discussion should be those applicable to *his*, not his subordinates', job. Second, all may make contributions which are not immediately obvious. One may be the "brainstorming" type who comes up rapidly with many stimulating and original ideas. Others may be hard-headed and objective and make the group do a rigorous job of sifting ideas. In short, it is not only available technical knowledge which is important; contributions to the process of decision making are also relevant and critical.

In the man-to-man situation, it is clear that sharply defined lines of responsibility are necessary because the advancement processes demand it. Two factors are important in that situation for making one's competence visible: the magnitude of one's responsibility and the definition of one's functions in such a way so as to ensure a successful record. Each man tries to enlarge his areas of responsibility, in the process encroaching upon another's territory. It is also in his interest to obtain, from his superior, decisions which set goals for him that are more easily obtained, in that way enabling him to attain an excellent performance record. One consequence of this power struggle is that each department or operation must be staffed for peak loads, and job responsibilities and boundaries must be very explicitly defined. No one dares let anyone else take over any part of his activity temporarily for fear that the line of responsibility will be moved permanently.[4]

By way of contrast to this, Likert has described a quite foresighted application of a participative group method.

In another large company, the president is making skillful use of what might well be called "anticipatory management" to help develop and strengthen the . . . organization. Before a problem occurs or before it becomes serious, he stimulates his organization to think about and devise strategies to cope with it. For example, prior to the time when the impact of the 1957–1958 recession hit his organization, he had already drawn the attention of his upper and middle management to the likelihood of a recession. As probability of a recession became more evident, he and his own work group considered what steps could be taken to minimize the adverse effects of the recession and what to do to keep costs to a minimum. They decided to take the problems to lower levels of management through work-group channels. They put before each management work group the necessity for reducing costs, but emphasized that it be done in ways which would not weaken the organization. As a result of these discussions, the organization made sufficient cuts in costs to stay well below its reduced income. The savings were sufficient to enable the company to make capital expenditures during the recession at favorable prices and thereby to strengthen the company's competitive position in the postrecession period.[5]

Influence and Control in the Participative System

It must be apparent that in a participative system all members have, in some manner and considerable degree, an ability to influence events by making their views known. There is an opinion, widely held by many persons in the management ranks, that allowing one's subordinates influence diminishes one's own influence. In this commonly held opinion, the influence pie is of a fixed size, and giving it to one person reduces the amount available to another.

In fact, however, research shows that a quite different pattern exists. As an example, consider a number of cars on a busy highway. There is, of course, a great deal of truth to the proposition that, if each driver felt responsible for his own driving behavior and exercised responsible care and attention to himself and his own car, even without attention to his neighbor, accidents would decrease. But would anyone seriously propose that this would be sufficient? It hardly seems likely. The careful driver knows that he must watch the man in front and the one in back, and not only those, but also the cars several ranks ahead, as well as those approaching from some distance behind. The greater the number of drivers who do this, the more the traffic flow is under control. Increasing the number of highway patrolmen, widening the berms or median strip, or passing stiffer violation laws are at best poor substitutes for this form of concerned influence.

Influence in organizations is in reality much like this. When all persons in a group feel responsible for that group's success and have an ability to influence events, the group's success is more likely than when the reverse exists. Similarly, effective organizations are, as systems, characterized by a presence of greater *total control* than are ineffective systems. Persons at all levels of high-performing organizations feel that they have, and do have, more say or influence over what goes on in their departments or units than do persons at those same levels in organizations which perform poorly. Fewer things are likely to be left to chance, fewer critical factors are likely to be overlooked, and fewer sudden errors are likely to go unchecked when members at all levels feel responsible and have an ability to do something about it, i.e., influence it.

It is important to note in this context that it is not the motivational consequences alone which are at issue. It is, in addition, the simple error proneness of the autocratic system which presents itself to be judged, because the prerogative of deciding things unilaterally carries with it the privilege of being far more often wrong.

CHAPTER 4

Motivational
Properties of the System

An organization that wishes to provide a climate which is encouraging, rather than discouraging, must so structure its policies, tasks, procedures, and conditions that two things are done. First, the organization must make it highly likely that it will be a success in the market place, that it will receive from the buying or supporting public those resources which will make it possible to meet its members' economic and social needs. Second, it must reach that end-state by a route which provides to its members a sense of accomplishment, fulfillment, satisfaction, and pleasure in their attainment.

In the long run, enterprises which are not an economic success do not survive, and the inherent challenge of their tasks is irrelevant. However, for at least some period of time, organizations can be a success in a profit and loss sense, but a miserable failure in the eyes of their members. (Ultimately, of course, this discrepancy is resolved, either by a responsive restructuring or by receivership.) This is, in fact, the pattern of all too many modern production organizations. Jobs have become so fractionated that they have lost both challenge and meaning, and the organization finds itself compensating in wages and benefits for imposed monotony and drudgery. The point is not that the organization could extract additional output for lower wages were it to do something other than what it does, but that, under conditions as they exist, no amount of money ever really suffices. What was required to induce members to produce for yet another two or three years becomes inadequate for the prospect of enduring it in the period beyond. Compliance may be purchased, but motivated cooperation and loyalty are never for sale.

It is instead the situation which meets both the members' needs and the organization's requirements which will be, in the long run, motivationally effective. To understand this issue more fully, we must distinguish among three different sets of forces or conditions: the needs of individuals (those things that the individual himself wants or desires), the goals of groups (those attainments that the group as such is truly committed to), and the objectives of organizations (those subparts of the total task which must be met by groups if the whole task is to be accomplished). For organizations and individuals alike, the problem is the alignment of these three. The most motivationally "right" situation is one in which these coincide or overlap, that is, where the needs of members are met by the attainment of goals which fulfill the required objectives. Organizational situations are motivationally inadequate where these do not synchronize.

Individuals do on occasion find themselves part of a group which is committed to goals which do not meet their needs; more often groups become committed to goals which do not match organizational objectives. In at least the latter of these situations it is tempting to the management of an organization to attribute the blame to members as individuals, to the vagaries and contrariness of human beings. In point of fact, however, such a situation nearly always reflects inadequate organizational management processes, because one of management's principal tasks is to create precisely that set of conditions and processes which prevent this from happening.

The desires and the needs of individuals are not stable and unchanging, nor are the objectives of organizations. The desires of individuals grow and change as they interact with other individuals. In the same way, the objectives of organizations change continually to meet the requirements of changed technologies, changed conditions, and changes in the values of society. In every organization, therefore, there is an unending process of examining and modifying both individual desires and organizational objectives.[1]

To be highly motivated, each member of the organization must feel that the organization's objectives are important, that its mission, whatever it may be, is of genuine significance. He must also feel that his own particular job contributes in an important manner to the organization's attaining its objectives. He should see his job as challenging, meaningful, and important. The likelihood of his viewing the organization's objectives and his own job in this light is heightened when the work goals of the group to which he belongs are set by a participative process that includes him, and when the objectives themselves are assembled or integrated in ways that best fit those goals and member needs.

Many organizations do in fact have objective-setting procedures—procedures for arriving at next year's performance objectives, for example—that reach well down into the lower echelons. The problem with such programs often is that they are not truly participative. They amount, instead, to the assignment of more or less arbitrary quotas, at best with a bit of arm-twisting to obtain a superficial acknowledgment from the person or group for whom they are set.

What typically accounts for apprehension at making the process more participative? Principally, it is the fear that employees, if truly involved in setting goals for themselves, will set them ridiculously below an acceptable level. Perhaps visions come to mind of events in the last round of contract negotiations, in which what was felt by the company to be legitimate labor-saving innovation was perceived by the union to be a speed-up effort. It might well be, let us acknowledge, that a firm with labor and employee relations of that kind would undergo a disaster if it established participative objective setting. Relationships, confidence, trust, loyalty, and a feeling of commitment to the organization are at such low ebb that the result of greater latitude could easily be greater lassitude. But the point really is that the disaster is already there, simply looking for a place to happen!

Motives Tapped by the
Organization's Policies and Practices

Organizations may, by their policies and basic practices, bring into play a wide variety of different forces relating to or affecting human motives which range well apart on a crude scale. At one end of the scale are those motives such as fear of physical, psychological, or economic insecurity and the desire for status and for power, that is, a desire to be seen as more important than others. At the other end of the scale are those motives whose emphasis is more positive, such as desires for achievement, affiliation, or esteem (the desire to be respected and valued for one's personal capability, qualities, or talent).

Let us first consider fear, a motive which we acquire early in life as a learned anticipation of punishment. Fear, like its more basic counterpart, is never associated with learning what *to do*, but rather what *not* to do (i.e., what to avoid).

This being the case, what is it that an organization which relies upon fear as a force in motivating its employees hopes to accomplish? Basically it hopes that members will learn to *avoid not doing* what they are told. In other words, the sequence of events which it hopes will occur takes somewhat the following form:

> *"Directive A, from your superiors, will tell you what to do."*

The organization presumes that the learned reaction will be:

> *"When I hear Directive A, I must avoid not doing what it calls for."*

However, the reaction really learned is the following:

> *"When I hear Directive A, I must avoid being caught not doing what it calls for. I must avoid being held responsible for the nonexistence of Directive A's outcomes."*

With diligence by the organization, this piece of learning will be indelibly internalized by the members, but is this what the organization really desires—a place where no one is ever *caught* in the dereliction of duty, a situation where not being responsible is developed to an ingenious art?

If fear is an ineffective motivator, interpersonally volatile and as likely to turn on its wielder as serve his purposes, desire for status is little better. At the outset, let us acknowledge that differences in actual status are inevitable. One cannot realistically conceive of a human social organization in which such differences will not ultimately come to exist. Complicated objectives require specialization and division of labor. These in turn require coordination, direction, and supervision, and all of these lead to differences in position. Some positions will become more powerful than others, and different amounts of status will accrue to the holders of these positions. It is not the *fact* of status, but the inordinate craving of members for it and its systematic use by the organization as a method of motivating its membership that cause difficulty.

The reason for this may not immediately be apparent. Status is a *comparative* thing; the desire for it is a desire to be "better" than others, or for others to be "worse" than oneself. One can gain status by outrunning one's fellows, but one can gain it equally as well by slowing or depressing them. Status does, of course, ordinarily come to those who succeed; but it can as easily be arrived at by causing others to fail. In many ways, in fact, the latter is the easier route. The person who shares all information, who passes quickly to his peers the latest productive innovations which he encounters, so that their contribution to the common goal can equal his own, is less likely to attain a status markedly greater than that of his fellow members. On the contrary, the status prize is more likely to go to the man who takes the situations and experiences to which he is given access by the organization and bends them to his personal benefit. He withholds vital information from others, so that his knowledge and accuracy are greater, theirs less; he keeps new ideas and methods to himself, retaining for his status account assets which rightfully should have gone, through the sharing, to the organization as a whole.

An equally destructive but perhaps more subtle effect occurs, however. In the status race, a number of losers are created for each person who wins. For the same reasons that attainment of higher status adds to a man's feeling of worth, receiving a lower status reduces it. Persons repeatedly or continually in the latter situation characteristically become alienated from the organization or situation which led to it, and become either hostile or apathetic, a state of affairs which can hardly be considered useful by an organization. In this way, as in the more tangible one mentioned above, the organization shortchanges itself when it relies upon status differentiation as a motivator.

All that has been said about status is equally true of power. One need only substitute *power* for *status* in the preceding paragraphs.

In the accomplishment-oriented world of work, success is rewarded, failure is not. Individuals can become focused upon either of these. The person who is motivated primarily by a fear of the punishment that failure brings often selects as his announced aims things so trivial and easy that there is practically no possibility that he can fail, or things so preposterously difficult that no one can blame him, in the light of his "heroic" goal, for the failure that is highly likely to occur. The person who is motivated by a need for achievement, on the other hand, selects high but reasonable aims, goals of intermediate probability of success.[2] For this reason, his real accomplishments are likely to add up, over a period of time, to a greater amount. It is clearly in the organization's interests, therefore, to create conditions favorable to the latter, not those which make the former more likely. Furthermore, a considerable volume of research has shown that persons set their future aspirations in the light of their recent experiences. A successful accomplishment leads to the setting of goals somewhat higher on the succeeding occasion; failure leads to their reduction.

An organization that wishes to maximize the likelihood of its overall success will therefore create, by its policies and practices, those conditions most likely to lead to success experiences, since these experiences will, in their own right, tend to lead to even higher aspirations with attainable goals. Of course this means that the organization will not demand more of its members than physical resources make possible; it will provide its members with those tools, materials, and pieces of technical information which are required to do the job well. As technology becomes more complex, however, it will do something more: it will build that kind of organization which encourages the pooling of knowledge and talent in ways likely to maximize high quality decisions and coordinated effort. Drawing upon the material of earlier chapters, we may say that the productive organization will draw upon the resources of effective groups, linked together in ways likely to maximize the flow of both information and product, and it will so build those groups that they are participative. It will do these things, at least in part, because, under conditions where all can make their informed contributions, where all can help prevent costly errors, events will be subject to a greater degree of control, and the greater success which results will enhance motivation.

Just as fear of failure has its positive counterpart—hope of successful accomplishment—so does desire for status have an analogous, but positive, motivational counterpart. The desire for esteem and to be valued helps to build, for many of the same reasons that the need for status serves to destroy. Esteem consists of one's worth in the eyes of one's colleagues, peers, subordinates, and superiors. It is tied, not to the position that one occupies, but to one's personal qualities of contribution, expertise, and warmth. These are measured, in work organizations, largely by verbal and physical behavior of others toward oneself, and they originate in the behavior that one directs toward others on behalf of a common goal. The person who shows to others by what he says and does, in visible, public, accessible ways, rather than covertly, that he (a) knows what he's doing, (b) understands both the technology and the situations in which it is operating, and (c) cares what happens to others whose contributions are also important to the common mission, gains in the esteem of his fellows. When esteem is the driving force in the organization, precisely the opposite happens as when status exists as the motivation: members are motivated to share information and know-how with one another, out of respect and liking for one another and because of a dedication to the overall objective whose attainment reflects upon them all. Information hoarding and one-upmanship are undesirable practices. The organization benefits from the problems which become solved and the improvements which are rapidly and widely adopted. Individuals identify with the organization, and feel a loyalty toward it.

The reader may at this point feel that a straw man has been contrasted with a utopian ideal. It has not: research conducted in a number of organizations over a period of years shows a pronounced tendency for this difference in motivational practices to characterize the contrast between poor performing and high performing units. Fear, status, and power politics very often typify the motivational base of the ineffective firm; an orientation toward achievement and a desire for esteem in the eyes of one's colleagues are very frequently characteristic of the effective organization.

CHAPTER 5

Communication: The Nerve Network of the System

The routes by which information flows, the volume and quality of the content which flows by those routes, and the efficiency by which the flow occurs are critical facts of the life of organizational systems. The more complex the organization is, in its structure and in its technology, the more critical this facet of its operation becomes. With a flow that is less than efficient, the organization's subunit efforts become uncoordinated; the absence of an information flow leads to paralysis and, with time, to the demise of the system. It is especially critical, therefore, that the organization concern itself with the flow of information upward, laterally, and downward.

Accurate downward communication is a condition highly prized in most organizations. Training courses in "ways to communicate with your subordinates" have been an area of

special emphasis for a number of years throughout the industry. Complicated and expensive systems are often designed
and introduced so that the organization may be more certain
than it otherwise would be that orders, priority shifts, and
policy changes are transmitted downward rapidly and accurately. Despite these efforts, most organizations experience
an inordinate frequency of orders not carried out, priorities
not appropriately shifted or not shifted quickly enough, and
policy changes characterized more by prolonged neglect than
by rapid compliance. The reaction of top managers to this
slippage is both human and understandable: since the mechanism is obviously adequate to the task of downward communication (it must be, because wasn't it built by some of our
best minds?), and since our directives were clear (who could
confuse what we have so specifically stated?), the solution
must lie in the negligence or perverseness of persons at lower
levels.

     What this view overlooks, of course, is the psychological
complexity of the communication process. Material must be
transmitted, to be sure, but it must be received, comprehend-
ed, and accepted as well. Negative feelings and attitudes—
hostility, fear, suspicion, and distrust—not only produce rejection instead of acceptance, but also often interfere with
comprehension of the message and even with its reception. In
at least some instances, the identity and reputation of the
sender, far from authenticating the message, leads instead to
the intended receiver's simply clicking his mental switch to
an "off" position. The ability of a downward message to get
through to its destination is heavily dependent upon the
sender's reputation for being credible, based upon the receiver's past experience with him. If most of the sender's past
messages have been harsh or painful, receiving new transmis-
sions from him will trigger avoidance on the receiver's part or
an effort by the latter to read into it what pleases him, not
what is necessarily there. If the sender's past messages have

been confusing or contradictory, his present ones will be filed in a dead compartment, for retrieval only if other evidence suggests consistency and relevance.

The more traditional a system is, the more it will tend to adhere to such practices as "management by exception," in which only important deviations from the established inertia of procedures and events are flagged and handled. The more meaningful a downward communication in such a system is, therefore, the more radical is the departure which changes its course. "Management by exception" also encourages an environment in which doing what one is supposed to do is expected and no cause for unusual note. Doing what one is *not* supposed to do, on the other hand, brings reprimand and unpleasantness. The prudent subordinate, therefore, confronted with any ambiguity, selects the course of doing nothing rather than the risk of doing the wrong thing. For this reason, response to communication in a traditional system tends to be quite conservative. It is this, not the personal shortcomings of subordinates, which produces comparatively inefficient downward communication in directive, autocratic organizations.

If downward communication, the importance of which is recognized by the organization, must contend with the obstacles just discussed, upward communication suffers from all of these and more. Top managers seem all too often to assume that some sort of "fail-safe" mechanism operates beneath them, that the system is constructed in such a way that sudden shifts, goofs, or deviations from specifications are, at least for the most part, automatically noted and corrected, or brought to their attention. However, painful evidence available firsthand to many top executives should at least cause uneasiness about this, if not demonstrate its being almost untenable as an assumption. Too often the first evidence of a malfunction in the system comes after, not before, the firm's product has reached the customer's hands. Carbon monoxide

does enter the passenger compartment, and rat hair *is* found
in the candy, despite the belief that errors far less serious
than this are caught and brought to the attention of management by a carefully designed operating system.

Efforts to augment the upward flow of information are
unfortunately often rather primitive. Reliance is placed upon
a suggestion system, inaugurated perhaps with a fanfare, but
soon deteriorating to the status of a dust-covered drop box
faced with a torn and yellowing poster upon which the disenchanted have scrawled their more pointed recommendations. Much is also often made of the "open door policy," a
stratagem which Likert has described with considerable accuracy.

> The policy that the boss always has his door open
> sounds fine, but unless a subordinate is about to resign,
> he is not likely to go through that open door to suggest
> that his superior is handling the work in ways that are in-
> efficient, is creating unnecessary difficulties for his sub-
> ordinates, or is unfair or unreasonable. Moreover, the
> worse the situation, the more difficult it is for a subordi-
> nate to communicate these facts to his chief. Most sub-
> ordinates have learned to study their superior and tell
> him only what will please him. This "yessing" the boss
> may misinform him, but it keeps the subordinate out of
> hot water and may result in his being rewarded. Even on
> "important things about the job," subordinates feel
> much less free to discuss these matters with their boss
> than the boss realizes. . . .[1]

It is a simple fact of organizational life, therefore, that
upward communication is likely to be no better than downward communication, and that the discrepancy between the
two is likely to increase, not decrease, as they both become
less effective under more autocratic forms of management.
The executive who feels perplexed and frustrated about the

seeming inability of those beneath him to hear, understand, and implement his directives, therefore, has little ground for comfort: it is likely that the upward flow of information upon which he is in part basing his directives is even worse than the downward flow whose inefficiency is causing him concern.

Like downward communication, communication upward is likely to be enhanced where there is created within the organization, particularly by groups at upper levels of the hierarchy, a climate which encourages it. Ability to communicate with clarity is certainly a necessary skill, and the effective organization makes sure that its members have that skill or an opportunity to acquire it if they lack it in some measure.

It is at least as important, however, that the organization demonstrate by its pronouncements, policies, and by the behavior of its managers at all levels, that it actively seeks the inputs and views of those at lower levels. Downplaying status distinctions aids this process, as does encouraging openness and expression of divergent views.

An ability to accept and cope constructively with criticism from one's subordinates also helps. Not only does it serve to increase the frequency with which innovative ideas surface, it also helps increase realism in the perspective which top managers have of the nature of operations below. Very often, for example, the most productive managers in the firm will be located at remote spots, and their corporate superiors will draw conclusions about the managerial styles of these highly effective persons on the basis of their own encounters with them. Likert describes a typical case:

Typically their highest-producing division or department often is at some distance from corporate headquarters. The manager of this division or department visits headquarters periodically and may from time to time express disagreement with the corporate staff concerning the effect of a particular policy or principle upon the productivity of his department. He usually holds firmly to his view and insists that he be permitted to operate his department in accordance with those principles and policies which he feels are essential in achieving high productivity, even though they deviate from the policies set by the corporate staff. He is seen as a man of strong conviction and great firmness. He is recognized as holding high performance goals for himself and his department. . . . Their conclusion is reasonable: he must be urging his subordinates to reach high performance goals with the same pressure and unequivocal firmness he uses in dealing with headquarters on matters of policy and on the principles and methods to be used in managing his department. He is seen to be a manager who, with high performance goals, achieves them through firm hierarchical pressure.[2]

In fact, however, he is likely to be a more participative manager than this view of him suggests, particularly as he has built a stellar organization. For his superiors, an ability to consider his criticisms constructively will aid them in distinguishing his behavior toward his superiors from his behavior toward those subordinate to him, which may exhibit a very different pattern.

Perhaps the most important component of an efficient communication system, however, is the building of effectively functioning, interlocked, overlapping work groups. It is in the strength of such groups that communication—upward, downward, and laterally—succeeds or fails. The properties of groups which lead them to have this quality have been discussed at some length in an earlier chapter and need not be repeated here. The reasons that they have this value to the system, and the role they play within it, deserve discussion.

The character of behavior and relationships within the

group determines the extent to which information will be shared, innovative opportunities brought to light, and potential pitfalls examined. For this reason, it has a great deal of influence upon the extent to which higher echelons are aware of potential problems before they become critical. The more participative stance by the supervisor that is necessary for such groups to be created and maintained is likely to improve downward communication as well. In addition to these positive impacts, effective groups enhance lateral communication because they serve to redefine the aims and objectives of the members from "what is good for my department" to "what is good for our whole operation, or for the entire company." Fulfilling the mission, not maintaining personal or parochial prerogatives, becomes the guideline, and because this is the case, members feel free to communicate with persons in other command lines when the need presents itself.

Where a work group is ineffective, communication at and through that point in the organization tends to break down. It is true, of course, that organizations may, like the human body in response to the removal of a small section of a blood vessel, attempt to compensate for this blockage by building bypass routes along which information may travel. These are at best makeshift, however, and the organization can never be quite as effective as it would be if the group in question were to become an effective work team.

One final observation deserves mention: just as individuals and groups have an effect upon communication, so does the flow of communication affect the groups which make up the system. No group can effectively perform its task if it lacks information about the relationship of that task to operations in other parts of the system. Upper level groups cannot make effective decisions if denied the information pertinent to those decisions stored in the experience and heads of persons at lower levels. Lower levels can scarcely implement upper-level decisions that are nonsensical because they bear only a partial resemblance to reality. Beyond these things, an organization, by its behavior in sharing information with its membership, says to the individual members that it trusts and respects them. In doing so, it enhances their motivation to accomplish the objectives because it adds to, rather than detracts from, their loyalty to the organization and their identification with it.

CHAPTER 6

Coordination and the Linking-Pin Function

Coordination amounts to nothing more nor less than keeping operations that are functionally or organizationally distinct, but interdependent, in gear with one another. The supply of fabricated parts going to an assembly operation must be adequate without being excessive. Production capability must be sufficient to fulfill sales orders, and marketing must sell products which the plant is capable of making. Where there are few persons or units, and operations are relatively simple, the task of coordination is fairly easy. Where large numbers of members work in many different units on complex tasks, the job becomes quite demanding. A simple example serves to illustrate this fact.

Seth ran a harness shop, at the turn of the century, with the help of an apprentice, handyman, and general factotum named Sam. Seth gave the orders, because he owned the shop, leather, and awl, knew what was to be done and when, and had every material, tool, and order within eyesight. For his part, Sam did what he was told, in some measure simply because that was the way things always had been, and partly because Seth could turn him out into the street if he did not.

Seventy years later, things are different. Seth's harness shop now makes fashionable leather jackets and belts; it employs one or two thousand persons producing leather and plastic materials in a large facility. Seth's great-grandson has a voice in affairs of the firm, but he is one shareholder among a great number. Sam's descendants work there, but they are much better educated and far more economically secure. Seth's unilateral form of management has evolved to a line-and-staff organization, characterized by lines of authority and chains of command.

In his bygone simple shop, Seth's behavior and Sam's response were consistent with what we call "traditional" or "classical" management practices. Based as they are upon a simple, economic-man theory of motivation (which in Sam's day and circumstance was perhaps a rather valid view), these practices rely upon the authority to hire and fire and follow the principle that a person can have only one superior and should be given orders by him and him alone.

This small illustration is not different from the development pattern of many, or even most, firms today. There is usually great pride in the distance that the company has come since Seth's day, yet there remains a commitment in theory to some of Seth's methods of management. In theory, when a unit well down in the hierarchy encounters a problem whose solution involves another unit at the same level in another command line, that problem is transmitted upward in the branching maze until it reaches that junction called a common superior. He then makes a decision, which flows down through the other line to the troublesome unit. To counsel him in these decisions, the manager may employ staff units with specialized knowledge. They are advisory, however, and the decision is his.

The thoughtful reader will certainly, and correctly, say that nowadays the system seldom works this way. There is much truth to the old observation that, if employees want to bring an operation to a complete standstill, they have only to abide strictly by rules such as this. Superiors at all levels would soon be swamped in resolving disputes, some of them petty and all of them so far out of their range of sight and familiarity that decisions would come forth painfully, slowly, or not at all.

What happens, of course, is that a second set of decision-making channels is created, often informally, which keeps the organization functioning despite classical principles and rules. These channels are lateral, rather than vertical, and operate ordinarily without an authority base. The foreman who encounters a difficulty caused by a unit responsible to another command chain often simply goes to his counterpart in the other unit. The two of them then settle upon a decision which solves the problem. They may or may not inform their superiors of their action, depending upon its seriousness, duration, and possible repercussions. In similar fashion, one department head solves problems with another, and chiefs of different functions establish procedures for handling their interrelationship.

The most effective organizations have simply recognized this process, refined and developed it along group rather than man-to-man lines, and made it part of their acknowledged system of management. Decision-making responsibility has been pushed down to the lowest possible echelon, that group whose membership supervises all those affected. Matters which affect persons or operations in one department and only that department are decided within the work group made up of the department head and his immediately subordinate supervisors. Issues relevant only to one group of work-

ers and their foreman are decided at that level. The company
president, rather than spending his time as a superdirector,
dabbling in the work of each of his vice-presidents and in effect duplicating their efforts, is freed, as are superiors at all
other levels, to plan for the future. Instead of constantly un-
tangling his subordinates' past difficulties, he is free to anticipate tomorrow's demands, next month's requirements, and
next year's needs for his entire area of responsibility.

Managers accustomed to the man-to-man handling of coordination problems often phrase a question in approximately the following vein:

> What in the deuce is more efficient about having 10
> men—my subordinates—spend two hours in a meeting
> making a decision that I myself could make in 15 min-
> utes? And it seems to compound itself, since each of them
> has 10 subordinates, more or less, who will be similarly
> doing *their* jobs. This seems to amount to having 111
> men take eight times as long as they should to do the
> jobs of 11, and I fail to see how this makes for more ef-
> ficient coordination!

There are at least a half dozen points to be made in response to this legitmate question.

1. Decisions made by participative groups are better understood and more wholeheartedly accepted by those
   who must jointly implement them. Many coordination problems will therefore be prevented by a process which involves these subordinates. If each of
   these nonoccurring problems had taken all of them
   only 15 minutes to unsnarl (which is unlikely), the
   time will have been recovered.
2. The process also redefines the matter of subordinates'
   loyalty and to whom or what that loyalty is owed; it
   will now be a joint commitment to the welfare of the

superior's whole area, not just to their personal bailiwicks, and they will be more motivated to alert a colleague to impending trouble in this area than they would if their own reputation for running a comparatively smooth operation were in part created by his having trouble. Again, coordination problems will in part be prevented.

3. Coordination issues that are handled unilaterally, regardless of the knowledge and skill of the handler, are likely to be less well handled than when several heads pool their insights. Individuals are human, after all; even the most capable persons become fatigued, distracted, and overburdened. In such situations, coordination problems are likely to recur and require repeated solution. It is simply more efficient for several persons to solve it once and for all, than for one person to solve it repeatedly.

4. As groups like this become more and more effective, the meetings will be much shorter and more efficient for a number of reasons. For one thing, members will acquire much greater familiarity with what each of them means by his words and expressions and will spend less time trying to find this out in each session. For another, since competitive gamesmanship will no longer seem as important, they will feel less need to consume airtime simply to make their presence felt. The two hours, therefore, may ultimately amount to little more than the fifteen minutes which the individual superior would spend were he to handle all such problems unilaterally.

5. As group members become closer to one another and more effective, fewer of the coordination issues will actually have to be discussed and explored in depth by the entire group. There will emerge instead an "implied consensus," the situation in which any one of

them can handle at least minor coordination problems as they arise, on behalf of the whole group, simply because he knows exactly how they feel about
particular matters. He can simply brief them on it at
the next meeting.

6. Finally, no group is an island, especially at the upper
levels of the organization. The more top managers invest themselves in handling coordination problems at
this level, the less time managers and groups below
must spend in attempting to handle the problems of
unclear objectives, confusing or contradictory decisions, and garbled communications. The time invested
will be more than recovered at those lower levels.

The Linking-Pin Concept

Linkage is an important aspect of the coordination process.
Although the term may appear obvious in its meaning, as
used in the present instance it means primarily that in a
complex organization the efforts of one subsegment of the
organization supplement or complement, and do not counteract or confound, those of another. They supplement in those
instances in which units produce independent, additive increments of product or service, as, for example, in each of
twenty paperboard plants producing the same products for
twenty different marketing regions. They complement where
units produce interdependent increments, for example, in
parts fabrication and assembly plants in an overall production
line operation. They counteract or confound where the efforts
of some units operate to the disadvantage of others. An illustration of this is the situation in which one paperboard plant
might begin to market surreptitiously, through its customers
and their subsidiaries, into the region of a sister plant. Another example, drawn from an instance in which units should

be complementary, would be the situation in which a parts plant produces too few components to meet the assembly plant's needs, or perhaps where it sells components to a competing firm's assembly operation during a period of short supply.

Linkage does not mean that the objectives or targets envisioned by the firm (regardless of the manner in which they were set) merely exist on paper. It means that the goals set and internalized by the firm's subunits, and which serve as *means* to those objectives, in fact sum up to the objectives, and that work efforts do in fact attain those goals. Linkage is thus a process of continuous monitoring, an assurance of good mutual fit of the efforts of subunits.

A great deal of research indicates that several conditions enhance the likelihood of effective linkage. One condition is quite fundamental, since it concerns the very way in which the organization is structured: linkage appears to be best where the organization consists of a meaningfully integrated network of *overlapping* groups.

There is nothing "magic" in this. It has simply to do with a fact recited earlier: when a number of individuals develop close bonds with one another and truly commit themselves to reaching a common goal, they are very likely to reach it. When each member knows that the others are counting heavily upon him to do his part, and when he values them highly as "his group," he will be more likely to do all in his power to meet his obligations.

In an organization constructed of participative groups more of this kind of commitment will therefore be involved and, within each group's area of responsibility and activity, there will be a greater frequency of products or services being delivered in appropriate quantity, quality, and kinds than where each man is responsible only to his organizational "maker." There will similarly be far fewer instances in which carelessness and maliciousness determine outcomes.

Where an organization consists of overlapping groups of the kind described, each person above the bottom tier (e.g., hourly employees) and below the top man (e.g., the company president) belongs to more than one group. He is simultaneously the superior of the group below and a subordinate in the group above. If the groups are effective, he has influence in both. The more participative both groups are, the more he is able (and likely) to influence his peers and superior in directions which square both with the real situation and facts which confront his subordinate group and with the needs which his subordinates feel. At the same time he has greater *real* influence with his subordinates, has greater credibility with them, has more "in the bank" upon which to draw. He is therefore better able to align their commitments to the requirements which his superior's group has established. Each group, superior and subordinate, has, through his common membership, greater positive impact upon the other; the analogy of two bits of magnetized iron, attracting each other with a firm bond when alignment occurs, is pointedly appropriate.

Several requirements for effective linkage are obvious from this discussion. One of these requirements is the existence of an overlapping group structure; a second is that the groups which overlap be effective groups, that is, groups which by their participative character encourage cohesiveness, lateral influence, and real downward influence. The third requirement is implicit, but deserves specific mention: the groups must be such that genuine upward influence is possible. When the supervisor, who, by his dual membership, is a linking pin in the system, has an ability to influence his own superior within the process of the upper group, linkage is possible and likely. If he lacks that ability, little linkage will occur. His efforts to build a committed group among his subordinates will falter because of a demonstrated inability on his part to deliver from the larger organization in a way that will meet their needs.

Certain aspects of linkage are not apparent from a statement of its basic characteristics, however. It has, in addition, certain systemic properties that must be mentioned. Perhaps most important of these is the fact that linkage is a more critical matter at higher levels of the organization than at lower, for the simple reason that the policies produced, decisions made, and objectives set at those levels affect a greater number of operations and persons than do similar efforts at lower levels. The vice-president who, because he is poorly linked within the group formed by his peers and the company president, misreads and misunderstands their signals, is likely to send his whole area of the organization veering off the intended course. A floor foreman has a similar effect only upon his nonsupervisory subordinates.

Another important systemic property of linkage is closely tied to the condition just mentioned. Where subunits of an organization are highly interdependent, linkage tends to acquire much more the character of being wired "in series," that is, it becomes an all-or-none form of connection. Poor linkage of one subunit to the rest and to the overall system can result in its doing its job poorly or in its doing a different job entirely from the one which the system envisions. Where their separate accomplishments are greatly dependent upon each other, an error of this kind effectively shuts the system down. In such a situation, an organization which relies upon single linkages runs a great risk. Effective organizations for this reason often build in multiple linkages, by such mechanisms as task forces, ad hoc groups, staff groups, and the like. In addition, superiors may from time to time hold meetings across more than one level of hierarchy. In this way the superior can note any breakdown in the linkage process, by observing whether subordinates of one of his own subordinates are reluctant to talk, never question any policy or procedure, give evidence of being fearful, or appear uninformed or misinformed. When this happens, the superior may wisely conclude that he has a job to do of coaching one or more of

his subordinates, or that his own efforts at building a well-
linked group of immediate subordinates are in some way inadequate.

More Complex Linkage Processes

The traditional concept that the line has the authority and
that staff is only advisory is breaking down increasingly as
technical processes and other problems become more complex. In many companies staff persons and units are exercis-
ing more influence than the line, simply because they possess
high degrees of expertise in highly sophisticated technical
areas. Often, one small work group of technical experts exerts more influence on an important decision than does the
company president. As one might expect, this frequently
causes serious friction and conflict.

The practices of the more effective organizations suggest
that a solution to this problem lies in having the line build
the kind of structure of overlapping groups, with effective interpersonal, communication, decision-making, and influence
processes, which has been outlined in the preceding pages.
Staff units can aid in this process by encouraging the establishment of, and by participating in, joint staff-line groups
and committees. In this manner there is at least a perceptibly
greater likelihood that all relevant parts of the organization
can contribute fully from their specialized knowledge and
skills. The contributions of line and staff will, of course, vary
with the problem and with the resources which each pos-
sesses.[1]

Where a superior sees his job in its true light in a complex modern organization, he strives to build a group in
which the best possible decision gets made, rather than to
construct a situation in which he personally makes what he
feels is the best decision. In the process he builds a group

which does what the situation demands, not simply what he himself wants. When all supervisors and groups in an organization have this attitude, certain solutions to perplexing organizational problems become possible that are not otherwise feasible.

Perhaps most importantly, these conditions permit an answer to the functional specialization versus product or geographical decentralization dilemma, a problem which nearly every large firm increasingly faces. New knowledge and methods are being produced at a rapidly accelerating rate. The capacities of human beings have an absolute limit, however, and making use of these new increments of knowledge and method pushes organizations toward increased functional specialization. Furthermore, the lower unit costs inherent in large-scale operations reinforce this movement.

Marketing and servicing of different product lines in different geographical regions, combined with an increasing urgency for lower distribution costs, pushes simultaneously in the direction of decentralization. In some instances both needs may fortuitously be accommodated by strategically positioning several large facilities in widely separated locations. Even in these instances, however, it is likely that some of the advantages of specialization may be lost as operating cost requirements lead to the lopping off of some specialties that, although highly useful, are not absolutely necessary in each location.

In a detailed description of a means for attaining coordination in a highly functionalized organization, Likert refers to the requirements for reaching an integrative solution to this dilemma.

A satisfactory solution requires an organization which can have extensive functionalization and which can also resolve differences and achieve efficient coordination on a product or geographical basis. This usually will neces-

sitate effective coordination horizontally as well as verti-
cally. To meet these requirements, an organization will
need to have two or more channels of decision-making
and coordination, with at least one occurring via the
functional lines and the other via the product or geographical line. Many persons in such an organization will
have two or more superiors.[2]

The reader inclined to dismiss the possibility that an individual might be accountable within *two or more* lines of hierarchy should pause to consider what has been said in the
preceding pages. If the two groups to which he belongs are of
the kind already described, in which he has a measure of influence, there is nothing in principle to prevent his being an
effective member of each. In fact, his dual membership under
those conditions can help to guarantee the coordination that
is obviously needed in the complex situations to which the
functionalization-decentralization dilemma refers. A general
foreman, responsible through his departmental superintendent to the vice-president for manufacturing, may also hold,
as part of his total job with the company, a position as a
member of the team charged with developing a total strategy
for a new product line. In this latter position, he might well
be responsible to a product line general manager, who is in
turn responsible to a vice-president for product development.
As long as both groups are participative and allow him influence, he can serve to bring the aims, goals, and activities of
each more in concert with the other. Under these conditions,
he can be a force for creating innovative solutions which sat-
isfactorily meet the requirements and opportunities presented by the situations faced by both groups. The focus will not
be, as it would be were he simply the "representative" of a
functionally vested interest, merely obtaining a decision favorable to a particular work group, department, or function,
regardless of how damaging it is to the rest of the organiza-

tion. The primary objective of the decision making in both groups is, instead, to discover a solution which will serve the best interests of the entire organization.[3]

The joint involvement of line and staff in effective work groups and teams helps to alleviate at least one of the modern organization's perennial problems. The cross-functional team, or matrix, form of organization may well provide an answer to the more serious problem inherent in the divergent pressures toward specialization and decentralization. Both of these rely, as do more commonplace situations, upon the building of an integrated network of participative groups. Whereas unilateral influence produces a narrow focusing upon parochial aims, a structure of overlapping, effective groups pulls together toward a set of common objectives. Coordination occurs, therefore, by means of the linkage which this form of organizational structure provides; its absence makes it highly probable that the organization's efforts will not be coordinated.

CHAPTER 7

Supervision and Peer Group Loyalty

In the chapters to this point we have considered certain general organizational conditions whose nature in part determines the ultimate effectiveness of the organization. In certain ways, an analogy may be drawn between the organization and a colloidal suspension (such as gelatin), in which particles are held in place by molecular bombardment from the surrounding medium. The preceding chapters have been concerned with the medium; in the present chapter we turn our attention to the processes which go on within the particle itself, the focal group. (By "focal" we simply mean the particular group to which we turn our attention for consideration.)

Much has been made in previous pages of the fact that legitimacy of position is a rubber crutch, useful perhaps for maintaining one's balance during periods of slight organizational vertigo, or for truncheoning others into compliance, but an unreliable support for any serious journey. Appointment to a position does, however, provide one important characteristic to the supervisor: it places him in a position of high visibility. As a result, what he does—how he behaves and how he acts—looms much larger than the behavior of any other members, and he in this way "sets the tone" for the behavior of the other members who are his subordinates.

Supervision as a Relative Process

Occupying, as he does, a preeminent position, the supervisor's behavior becomes a causal condition, that is, a catalyst which initiates a chain of subsequent events. It would be a mistake, however, to assume a perfect correspondence. Consider the following hypothetically "pure" situation, containing no uncertainties:

> In situation A, supervisor B perceives a need for behavior C by him toward subordinate D, provides that behavior, and gets the predicted reaction E.

If supervisor-subordinate interchanges were as deterministic as this model implies, the problem of explaining the process and building a capacity for effective functioning in managerial roles would be indeed quite simple. We would need only to develop a "cookbook" of what to do in each circumstance.

Of course it is not as simple as this; a number of ambiguities enter into the calculation. For one thing, situations are often misunderstood, misread, or not read at all by the supervisor. What he perceives as a lack of motivation, for example, may in fact represent a temporary breakdown in information flow, or perhaps distraction caused by home or family problems. Second, supervisors are far from perfect in their ability to match a "corrective" behavior to the situation. Even if the situation is precisely what they believe it to be, they may prescribe the wrong act on their own part as the course of action to handle it. Third, even if the prescribed behavior is appropriate, there may well be a discrepancy between the amount or kind which the supervisor sees himself as providing and that which the subordinate views as having occurred. What appears to the supervisor to be a giant leap on his part may appear to the subordinate as a minor fluctuation in the former's customary pattern. Finally, even though the situation is correctly matched to it, and input is viewed in the same terms by both actor and recipient, the reaction by the latter may be different from what was expected. Values and expectations differ somewhat from one person to another; what is positively viewed by one may be a bit of effrontery to another.

That there are these potential sources of slippage should not be taken as evidence for despairing of any predictable connections. On the contrary, in most instances there is a reasonable fit between the supervisor's assessment of the situation and what really exists, and between the situation as he sees it and his prescription of behavior to fit it. Furthermore, values and expectations develop from experiences which persons share through memberships in common or similar groups and a common culture. General principles of supervisory leadership can be stated, therefore, and the *kinds* of behavior appropriate for *most* persons can be described. Considering for the moment only cultural differences, the situation may be illustrated by figure 1.

As this illustration suggests, there is probably a "core" of behaviors appropriate in all cultures. To this must be added, in each culture, those behaviors which are appropriate only to it. How large the core is in relation to the culture-specific areas is difficult to determine. In general, to measure behavior in a particular domain of supervisory leadership,

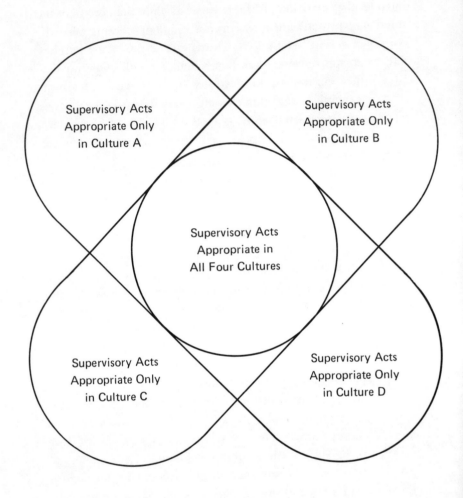

Supervisory Acts
Appropriate Only
in Culture A

Supervisory Acts
Appropriate Only
in Culture B

Supervisory Acts
Appropriate in
All Four Cultures

Supervisory Acts
Appropriate Only
in Culture C

Supervisory Acts
Appropriate Only
in Culture D

Fig. 1. SUPERVISORY ACTS APPROPRIATE IN ONE
AND IN SEVERAL CULTURES

reliance is placed upon material felt to lie within the common core. Recent evidence, in fact, suggests that the core may be much larger than one might initially imagine; items used to tap dimensions of supervisory behavior in the American culture have been found to tap them in very similar ways in two subcultures of Western Europe.

Despite this suggested commonality, supervisors should be aware that some differences will exist. Likert states this need for adaptability in the behavior of supervisors quite concisely.

> *The subordinate's reaction to the supervisor's behavior always depends upon the relationship between the supervisory act as perceived by the subordinate and the expectations, values, and interpersonal skills of the subordinate. . . . Supervision is, therefore, always a relative process. To be effective and to communicate as intended, a leader must always adapt his behavior to take into account the expectations, values and interpersonal skills of those with whom he is interacting.*[1]

The Principle of Supportive Relationships

A basic assumption about human motivation was presented in the first chapter: each of us has, in some degree, a need to feel that he is a worthwhile person, that his well-being is important and his contribution counts, and that he is respected and liked by those who are important to him. Experiences which a person has in the course of his organizational life, and the behavior of others toward him (especially behavior by his supervisor), produce a favorable reaction when they enhance that perception, an unfavorable reaction when they reduce or weaken it. Likert phrases this in very specific terms as a general principle which effective managers appear to employ in forming their supervisory styles.

> *The leadership and other processes of the organization must be such as to ensure a maximum probability that in all interactions and all relationships with the organization each member will, in the light of his background, values, and expectations, view the experience as supportive and one which builds and maintains his sense of personal worth and importance.*[2]

Although the specific ways in which effective managers implement this principle vary widely with their personalities, with the needs and values of the subordinates with whom they deal, and with the requirements of the situations in which they find themselves, there are certain areas of commonly agreed upon practice. In general, managers and supervisors who are supportive in their dealings with subordinates are approachable, rather than remote and aloof, are considerate of the feelings and needs of their subordinates, demonstrate that they trust them, take a participative stance toward their opinions and views, and provide them with adequate recognition for their accomplishments. We shall consider each of these subareas of supportive behavior separately, describe some typically supportive acts, and present occasional real-life illustrations drawn from an interview study of manager-agent relationships in a large insurance firm.

Approachability

The supportive supervisor is basically a friendly and unpretentious person. He is firm when firmness is called for, but not threatening or hostile. He talks with his subordinates at their workplace as well as his own, listens closely and patiently to what they have to say, and makes himself available when he is needed.

The unapproachable supervisor, on the other hand, often presents himself as rather dour; his face may be a grim, stony mask, and he rarely gives forth a smile or a really human comment. He frequently manages to have his subordinates talk with him on his own turf, while he sits safely behind his desk. He may subject subordinates to sitting idly, even at the outset of a prearranged appointment, while he finishes another task. During the conversation itself, such a supervisor may shuffle papers, sort folders, read correspondence, fidget in his chair, or repeatedly check his watch. Even worse is the wrist alarm, set to go off in mid-conversation, or the patently transparent telephone call from his own secretary reminding him that he has more important matters to which to attend. Many of these may be unconscious mannerisms; certainly few managers are guilty of them all. Collectively, however, they give the subordinate the uncomfortable impression of unapproachability and indicate to him that he is not important to this supervisor.

Consideration

The supportive supervisor demonstrates by his behavior that he is interested in his subordinates as human beings, not simply as hands useful for getting the work done, or as impersonal cogs in a machine. He shows that he is sensitive to their feelings, mindful of their needs and interests, and concerned with helping them solve their problems. One young subordinate said of his manager,

> I think he really cares—that he really, sincerely cares what happens to me, and what my opportunities are, that this is foremost on his mind. He makes me feel that

where I'm going is a heck of a lot more important than where he's going.

This forms a striking contrast with

I don't know whether he takes us for granted, or whether he puts us in categories where he says, "Well, he'll only do so much, and he'll do it with a minimum amount of time on my part, and therefore, for the investment of time, this is a good investment. If I put in any more time, it will be a poorer investment." This is the only conclusion I can draw.

As this second example indicates, the inconsiderate manager is more likely to ignore the human feelings and needs of his subordinates. He is more likely to lapse into criticism of them for appearance, beliefs, or even ethnic background, ridicule that he alone may think is humorous. Also indicative of a nonsupportive posture is the scheduling of weekend and evening meetings or work, or setting unreasonable deadlines, without consideration for the subordinate's personal life or his family's needs. Finally, the inconsiderate supervisor often adopts the position that the subordinate's problems on the job are his own concern, and that he, the supervisor, is paid to punish or fire him if he does not solve them, but is not paid to help in their solution.

Participation

Supportive supervisors seek the involvement of their subordinates in issues affecting the latter's work lives. Much has been said about this in earlier chapters in a discussion about participation as a general condition within the firm. Little more need be said at this point except to reiterate that being supportive in part means that the supervisor seeks out his subordinates' views and ideas, attempts to put them to use, gives serious consideration to matters which they raise, and shares with them as much information as possible.

Supervisors who are not supportive behave in precisely the opposite way. They often simply announce decisions and changes that drastically affect the work lives of subordinates at the time at which they are to be implemented. They indicate their evaluation of the potential contribution of those subordinates by flatly ignoring it, and they provide no one with any more information than he absolutely must have to perform the task at hand.

Trust and Confidence

Supportive supervisors show that they have confidence in the integrity, ability, and motives of their subordinates. They demonstrate by their behavior that they have confidence that the subordinate can do his job successfully. They exercise general, rather than close, supervision, and they share information with their subordinates that will add to the latter's understanding of events which affect them, even to the sharing of somewhat sensitive though nonconfidential information.

Less supportive supervisors maintain a close surveillance over the work habits and product of their subordinates, often insisting that they personally review or revise even the most trivial matters. A secretary who has stopped for a moment to make a personal telephone call may suddenly find that her supervisor has dropped a great load of work on her desk, and that this becomes a recurring phenomenon. Managers who are mistrustful often refuse to allow anyone to make commitments on behalf of themselves or the unit, insisting that all such questions be referred to them personally. Aside from the costly delays which this causes, their lack of confidence in their subordinates is also reflected by the managers' unwillingness to share information, preferring instead to communicate quite selectively.

Providing Recognition

The supportive supervisor is careful to provide praise and recognition for a job well done. To the extent that he errs, he does so on the side of commission, rather than omission, since he probably is aware that deserved recognition builds new and higher levels of aspiration, that undeserved recognition builds felt commitments to "make it good," but that acknowledgment deserved but not given yields only a destructive outcome. He very scrupulously avoids attempting to claim the credit for himself at his subordinates' expense, and he treats mistakes as an opportunity for subordinates to learn, rather than as an occasion for punishment. An agent in an agency where providing effective recognition was felt to be particularly important described his manager in the following terms:

> He knows when everybody writes a case; he knows this daily. And he'll say to somebody, "Gee, that was a *dandy* you had!" or something like that. And these fellows are just elated to think that he would even notice. There's never an application written that he isn't right there to congratulate them, and, when the policies come back, well, "Here's your policy, and congratulations again."

A pointed contrast can be drawn to a similar agent in a situation in which the manager has the reputation of being distinctly deficient in supportive behavior.

> A classic example: during the months of January, February, and March, I wrote less than the total for a

very good month. Nothing was said. Now in one week of one month, I wrote the equivalent of those three months. Still nothing was said. No recognition. And then it turns out that this month was a good month. So the manager's conclusion will be, "Well, I knew he'd work it out!" I tell you, I was an edgy son-of-a-gun in March! Some others have gone through this too, and we draw our strengths from ourselves. We have to. But from that, each time it happens, you take a little bit of loyalty."

High Performance Goals

Just as he sets the tone of his subordinate group in the area of supportive behavior, the supervisor provides a cue to his group in the area of performance goals by his visibility. As the group's leader, he helps to provide and channel stimulation for the group. He is an important source of enthusiasm for the significance of the mission and goals of the group, and he discourages complacency and passive acceptance of the present. He makes certain that the tasks of the group are important and significant and difficult enough to be challenging and, by doing so, helps the members to become aware of new possibilities, more important values, and more significant goals. In this light, Likert cites evidence suggesting that it is necessary for a supervisor to have higher goals and higher aspirations for his group than he expects those subordinates to have for themselves.[3]

Positive enthusiasm of high performance goals is different from punitive pressure, however. Contagious enthusiasm does not consist of urging and exhorting subordinates to produce. They want to be stimulated and helped, but not nagged. Although this may appear to be a fine line, there are certain identifiable distinctions between the "pressure artist" and the supervisor with effective, high performance goals. This may

be seen most clearly in the ways in which the latter commu-
nicates his adherence to high standards.

For one thing, he gives his subordinates a reputation to
live up to. When he represents the group to other units, above
or to the side in the organizational hierarchy, he expresses his
faith in the group's capability and dedication to high performance. An interview respondent describes this in the following way:

> The confidence he has in his men is the thing that
> makes some of them very successful. They want to mer-
> it his estimate of them, and I think that is all-important.

He also helps them translate vague ambitions or aspirations into concrete objectives of short-term, long-term, and
intermediate range.

> He always tries to stress with everyone setting a cer-
> tain goal to work toward, and then a long-term goal,
> such as a yearly quota, being met by your intermediate
> monthly and weekly goals. He tries to work from what
> they want for themselves and their families as a living
> scale, and what they want to accomplish, and then
> works back from there. . . .

A third way in which the effective supervisor helps to
encourage high performance goals is by a process of recipro-
cation: he sets a personal example of hard, dedicated, selfless
effort on their behalf. This is described by a respondent in
the following fashion:

> He's always on the go, and you pick this up and want
> to emulate it. You feel he's doing such a good job for
> you that you feel guilty if you don't appreciate this by
> working hard yourself. He's just one hundred percent
> enthusiastic in everything he does. If you have a prob-

lem, he'll help you; you always know that you can depend on him. Well, if you have a man like that backing you, you feel like this, that if a man's going that far out for me, the only thing I can do to show him my appreciation is to get out and work. And you feel good in doing it.

Many highly effective managers have discovered in practice a fact which research has also shown, that care must be taken not to encourage the setting of goals that are unreasonably high. A manager described it in the following way:

> I feel that when an agent has a goal that's way out of line, or way beyond his accomplishment, he's hurting himself. He'll feel that, if he can't attain it, he's going into a slump.

An agent who has experienced the excessive climb rate and readjusted his pace describes it in this way:

> I get scared. It's like climbing a ladder; the first few steps are no problem. You get up in the middle, and you begin to question the height, and then you have to go up to the peak of the house, stand on the top of the ladder and reach out a little bit, and then you're scared that you really might fall. This is why I don't go up faster.

Another agent described the actual experience of a "fall."

> The manager is used to large cases. Hell, the average agent doesn't get those. The $100,000 case is the exception. He's bringing our sights up, but he's bringing them so goddam far up I can't see them. I mean, don't bring me from cloud one up to cloud nine: let's try for three, maybe four. But don't bring me to the twenty-second story from the second, because I'm gasping for breath,

and then, when I jump off, I fall 22 stories, and it's a rough goddam jolt, I'll tell you!

Marshaling Technical Resources

We will attach the gerund "marshaling" to the words "technical resources" to distinguish this next aspect of supervisory behavior from the mere possession, on the supervisor's part, of technical competence. Just as in tribal life the criterion of chieftaincy was a combination of those technical characteristics most obviously related to survival tasks, i.e., physical size and muscular strength for war and hunting, so there is a tendency to equate supervision in the modern world with personally having the greatest technical knowledge about the process involved. This is pointedly not the view to be described in these next pages; in many instances the least desirable candidate for appointment to a position of managerial responsibility is the person with the greatest technical competence in his task area. The brilliant scientist who is often oblivious of those around him, his vacuous stare indicating preoccupation at the moment with intricate calculations or concepts, scarcely has the interpersonal skills necessary to manage a human organization. An ingenious technician who regards administrative tasks as annoyances to be sloughed off will produce more chaos than accomplishment if given responsibility for directing a department. This is not to say that technical competence necessarily is negatively related to managerial capability; it simply suggests that there is not a perfect correspondence between personal technical know-how and the ability to get technical resources to the locations where they are needed and in the amounts and kinds required.

Likert describes this aspect of the supervisor's behavior in the following way:

The leader has adequate competence to handle the

technical problems faced by his group, or he sees that access to this technical knowledge is fully provided. This may involve bringing in, as needed, technical or resource persons. Or he may arrange to have technical training given to one or more members of his group so that the group can have available the necessary technical know-how when the group discusses a problem and arrives at a decision.[4]

The highly effective manager makes full use, therefore, of technical resources, but he does so in such a manner that motivation is enhanced rather than diminished, and favorable, cooperative attitudes created rather than destroyed. More specifically, he directs the work by seeing that the work to be done is planned and scheduled, that subordinates are supplied with materials and tools, that work activities are initiated, and by making certain that necessary technical information is made available to them. He makes certain also that each subordinate is well trained for his particular job, and endeavors to help subordinates gain promotion by training them for jobs at the next level. This involves giving them relevant experience and coaching them, whenever an opportunity arises. He coaches and assists employees whose performance is below standard, as well. This is illustrated in the following report of a supervisor of young agents regarding the on-the-job training which he provides:

Our job is to demonstrate it (a sales talk) to him and then give him a written sales talk, one that I have just given him. Then he learns it and gives it to me again. Then he will give it to my secretary, then he'll give it to the manager, and then he'll give it to his wife, until he has learned this, until it is not a "canned" sales talk, but it is the best way that he knows how to express the idea that he wants to get across. I help while he's doing this, if I can. Basically, we're trying to get the thought back first, the general thought, and I don't care if he misses a word. The first time around he can't do it—I couldn't do it—so he'll get stuck. I'll say, "Now, we're trying to get this point across," and he'll say, "Oh, yes," and he'll come up with it. And then he'll get stuck again, and I'll encourage him with, "That's fine; keep coming," and "Don't worry about it; it took me longer than it did you; it will take a little bit of time, a little bit of practice." I think that I can remember when I first started to learn the sales talk, and I didn't want to make any mistakes in front of my trainer. I was scared. Well, I think that most people feel the very same way, so consequently what I want to do is pull them out of that shell.

This is in distinct contrast to the recollection of an agent in another agency, where technical competence had not been so carefully built. In response to a question about the kind of systematic follow-up provided during his early months, he said,

It was what I call "management by exception." After I had had three or four bad months, someone jumped on his back, and then he jumped on mine. We might be in January, and he would give me very close, intense criticism of October. He didn't give me any help as to what to do in January. He still doesn't provide any supervision. He's not around, and he has the quality to be able to divorce himself from anyone's problems in the business. If you're down, there's an interim there that he doesn't realize it until the passage of time. And then it's all negative: he doesn't tell you how or what you should do constructively to improve. He tells you you're not making enough money, you aren't making enough calls, you aren't doing this, you aren't doing that, but never what you should do.

Although these illustrations are all in the area of training or coaching of technical skills, similar points could be drawn to such areas as scheduling and planning. In all of these, the supervisor's most effective posture is that of a helpful facilitator of the flow of work technology, not that of a puppeteer who pulls technical strings.

Group Methods of Supervision

Earlier chapters have discussed the necessity for thinking of the organization as made up of groups as basic building blocks, and for creating within the organization those participative decision-making, motivational, and communication structures which will provide a healthy climate within which those groups may function. The supervisor himself, within the focal group, has as a fourth basic component of his leadership behavior those acts which, taken collectively, comprise group methods of supervision.

The supervisor who uses group methods effectively develops his subordinates into a tightly knit group, and conducts the business of the group *in the group*. He does this by encouraging the members, and developing their capacity, in order to reveal and resolve any frictions, emotional tensions, and destructive rivalries. In place of hostile or apathetic relationships, he encourages them to develop warm, supportive, close ties to one another. He provides them with exposure to, and experience and training in, effective group processes of decision making and communication. He provides ample opportunity for members to express their thoughts to one another and to him.

He may, if he has the latitude in the situation within which the group finds itself, go an additional step: he may make the selection process itself a group activity. Where each has had a voice in selecting his fellow members, there is less potential recourse to subsequent feelings of not being responsible for another member's welfare and effectiveness. The fol-

lowing quotation from an agent in the interview study illus-
trates this point:

> Before an agent comes into our agency, at least in our
> office, and I think that this is agency-wide, everybody
> has a say, and, if we don't want him in, he doesn't come
> in. If we want him, he comes in. So if the guy fails, it's
> as much our fault as it is the manager's. (Interviewer:
> "Suppose you just don't like the guy, but everyone else
> does?") Well, if we've got a dissenter, we've either got to
> overcome the dissenter or the guy won't be coming in.

Developing close ties of the kind just described results in
a feeling of mutual responsibility and concern illustrated in
the remarks of a manager.

> Two months ago one of the agents had a bad cold,
> didn't take care of it, ended up in the hospital, and
> darned near died of pneumonia. At different meetings
> we were having we'd have a report and make a phone
> call for the fellows to see how he was. This wasn't show-
> ing off; we were genuinely interested in him. And of
> course it made him feel good. But I also think it made
> the fellows feel good, because that could have been
> them: we were interested!

Contrast this with the following examples in a setting in
which ties of that sort had not been built, or had been built
and subsequently allowed to deteriorate:

> There is a deep-seated and continuing "unmorale"
> situation here. This is like "unwork"—it's the reverse of
> morale, like there's none. There's no communication at
> all among the leading agents: everyone goes into his cu-
> bicle, and, if you have a hot idea, you make certain that

nobody else gets a look at it. We wouldn't share our knowledge, or our ideas, with any other agent in the business!

The former manager was a man's man; he could reach us. We had a little esprit-de-corps. But I'll tell you, if you ever want to see a dead esprit-de-corps chicken, well, we've got one here—the esprit-de-corps is lousy! It bothers me deeply, because I'm associated with the agency, and, as this cancer sets in, I'm bound to get some of it on me. It's impairing my effectiveness, and I know it. You should hear all the griping around here. It's a joke when they bring in a new guy: "Huh! I wonder how long he'll last!" "Who's gonna train *him*?" and so forth.

Beyond the simple building of close relationships, however, the supervisor who is effective in group methods of supervision builds a dedication to good, solid performance by encouraging the setting of team, as well as individual, goals. A manager describes the usefulness of this:

We do use goals, no doubt about it, and the main goal is an agency goal. Everybody recognizes that he has a part, and then it's more an agency goal than it is individual goals. We're working with fellows all the time; we have the Round Table as a goal for the agents that we think are capable of reaching it, and we do everything we possibly can to keep their sights on that. But those are not the problem agents; those are the agents who will run by themselves. It's the ones who don't have that much capability that you have the problem with, and we find they achieve more by a team goal than anything else. They'll get more excited about doing something for the team.

Not only a team goal, but mutual help to reach that goal, comes from the effective use of group methods of supervision.

(Interviewer: "Suppose you were top dog in this group because everyone else dropped off; would you be concerned about this?") Yes, I'd be concerned for them. I mean, that's one good thing about this agency: you can go to anyone here, the million-dollar producers or anyone, and they'll sit right down and give you new ideas to help you out. I think it goes back to the manager, really; he's got ways of motivating people to work for each other. (Interviewer: "How?") Well, by holding meetings often. You get to know the other guys, and you talk over each other's problems in the meetings.

And from a manager:

It may sound like a bunch of junk, but our fellows are really trying to help each other! In our C.L.U. study group, do you know who our instructors are? They're both C.L.U.'s. Do you know how much I pay them? Nothing! And yet every Saturday the group meets. Now, I realize that this isn't right, so with both of them I intend to do something especially nice for them for this, but I have purposely not done anything so far, because it would look as if I'm paying them for it. (Interviewer: "Did you ask them to do it?") I think it just sort of came out of another study group that we had. We had three C.L.U.'s, and they said, "All right, we'll help you."

As these illustrations suggest, the supervisor who is effective in group methods of supervision holds frequent meetings in which members may establish joint goals, make necessary decisions, explore mutual needs and possibilities for mutual help, and review progress to date. Likert describes a program of group-based development counseling and goal setting which has proved extremely effective in improving the performance of less experienced agents, but also useful with agents who have longer years of experience.

The group method of sales supervision in these offices grew out of a coaching system originated in the organization several years ago by a member of the headquarters sales management staff. He launched the coaching system when he recognized that more had to be done to help new salesmen, who had been carefully selected and extensively trained, to become successful. In each sales unit, the manager, or a supervisor, was asked to meet regularly in group coaching sessions with the salesmen who had less than two or three years' experience. The purpose of conducting the meetings in groups was to have each new man learn not only from the manager's analysis of that individual's sales performance but also from hearing the manager's analysis of the work of each of the other new men and from the coaching he provided them. After several months' experience with these group sessions, some managers noticed that the salesmen liked to join in the analysis and coaching process and encouraged them to do so. In some of the sales units, this led to a fundamental change in the process. The manager became aware that more was accomplished when he served as a chairman and group leader rather than as the coach. The process became one of group problem solving, group coaching, and group goal setting. Each member committed himself to the group and to the manager to meet the target which the group had helped him set.

The exact process of these group sessions varied appreciably from unit to unit but is likely to be about as follows: The salesmen meet regularly in group meetings. The number of men varies depending upon the number in the territory but usually does not exceed 12 or 15. They meet at regular intervals every two weeks or every month. As a rule, the sales manager or one of his sales supervisors presides. Each salesman, in turn, presents to the group a report of his activity for the period since the last meeting of the group. He describes such things as the number and kinds of prospects he has obtained, the calls he has made, the nature of the sales presentations he has used, the closings he has attempted, the number of sales achieved, and the volume and quality of his total sales. The other men in the group analyze the salesman's efforts, methods, and results. Suggestions from their experience are offered. The outcome is a valuable coaching session. For example, if sales results can be improved through better prospecting, this is made clear, and the steps and methods to achieve this improvement are spelled out. After this analysis by the group, each man, with the advice and assistance of the group, sets goals for himself concerning the work he will do, the procedures he will use, and the results he intends to achieve before the next meeting of the group.

The manager or supervisor acts as chairman of the group, but aside from occasional discussion of complex, technical matters, the analyses and interactions are among the men. The chairman keeps the orientation of the group on a helpful, constructive, problem-solving basis. He sees that the tone is supportive, not ego-deflating. He encourages the group to set high performance goals which will help each man realize his full potential.

Each salesman, as a consequence of the group meeting, feels a commitment to the group and his manager to do the work and achieve the results which he has set for himself. His motivation is often stimulated between meetings by members of the group who remind him of his goals and commitments if they see him lagging or failing to make the needed sales calls. Moreover, because of the group loyalty created by the meetings, a salesman can, if he needs it, obtain coaching on some problem or assistance on a case not only from his supervisor but also from the other salesmen who had discussed the problem or offered relevant suggestions in the previous meeting. Each salesman has available the technical knowledge and skills of his colleagues as well as that of his supervisor or manager.

Salesmen derive four important benefits from this kind of group meetings: (1) they set higher sales goals, goals which more nearly reflect their own potentiality; (2) they are more highly motivated to achieve these goals, and they obtain greater satisfaction from their accomplishment; (3) they receive more technical assistance in selling by obtaining help from both their superior and their peers; and (4) new appeals, new markets, and new strategies of selling, when discovered by any individual salesman, are shared promptly with the group and improved and perfected by them. Often this improvement is facilitated by experimental field testing between group meetings. Important skills are not bottled up in a particular individual but are rapidly shared and cooperatively improved.

These group meetings are effective when the manager (or supervisor) does a competent job of presiding over the interactions among the men. Appreciably poorer results are achieved whenever the manager, himself, analyzes each man's performance and results and sets goals for him. Such man-to-man interactions in the meetings, dominated by the manager, do not create group loyalty and have a far less favorable impact upon the salesman's motivation than do group interaction and decision meetings. Moreover, in the man-to-man interaction little use is made of the sales knowledge and skills of the group.[5]

In the preceding sections of this chapter, the conditions, principles, and practices of effective supervisors, as they have emerged from research findings, were described. These have been illustrated by quotations drawn entirely from one industry, insurance sales. Although it may be felt that the examples given are unique to the industry and the situations in which they occurred, they are not; each can be extrapolated to other situations.

A second hesitancy may stem from the feeling that it is one thing to describe, another to implement effectively. More will be said on the implementation question in a subsequent chapter. For the moment, it should be stressed that these behaviors must reflect a sincere interest on the part of the supervisor who displays them. Nothing reveals itself so quickly as a phony attempt at slick "human relations." This may lead some to believe that no implementation can occur prior to a long and painful process of self-examination by the supervisor. In some instances this is, of course, true. Still, although it may take some experience and practice for a supervisor unaccustomed to handling a problem-solving meeting or encouraging high performance goals with great skill, it requires no sudden "conversion" experience to convene such a meeting or attempt such encouragement. Nor does it take the ordinary man a profound confrontation with his values to demonstrate a little simple kindness or human concern to a subordinate. Acquiring the knack of doing it is, first and foremost, a task of simply *doing* it, and learning by the doing.

Finally, it is sometimes suggested that the behaviors described can be in some way divided up, such that a supervisor who is good on task dimensions, but poor on the interpersonal side, can "hire" someone with the reverse pattern to complement his own. The example often given is that of the combination of ship's captain and his executive officer, where, if the former is a tough-as-nails taskmaster, he must bring on board an executive officer who is warm and sympathetic. If the captain is by nature warm, however, he must have a taskmaster executive officer. It is the writer's view that this is incompatible with the principles expressed; both sets of skills must be held by the same person. If they are not, far from complementing one another, they cancel each other out. As a manager once expressed it, "I can no more hire an assistant to provide my subordinates with the support and closeness which they need than I could hire a lover for my wife!" Nor should he.

CHAPTER 8

The Organization as a
Social System

The organization with its properties which surround or en-velope a group has systemic character as Likert conceptual-izes it. There is in the concept of the organization the notion of a flow of events, from causal conditions through interven-ing processes to end results. An adequate understanding of the organization's systemic nature requires that we under-stand this flow for any separate group and for all groups as they exist in a constellation making up the whole. If groups in an organization were not interconnected, we could simply sum up their separate properties and have an understanding of the whole. In fact, however, end results from some groups form causal inputs for other groups; thus the flow of events is from group to group, as well as within any one.

For the single group, two basic types of causal charac-teristics are given preeminent status in Likert's thinking:

managerial behavior and those organizational conditions which reflect the basic structure of expectations, roles, policies, and practices of the organization as they relate to a particular group. These conditions are described in terms of the extent to which there is a structure of groups with overlapping membership, the extent to which information flows easily and accurately in all directions, the degree to which there is coordination among separate operations and units, the degree to which there is a participative decision-making structure, and the extent to which motivational forces generated within the system are positive and mutually reinforcing, as opposed to negative and conflicting.

More recently the term "organizational climate" has been applied to this array of conditions which affect the basic life of a group and which flow to the group's milieu from the output of other groups, particularly those above it in the hierarchy.[1] This use of the term differs somewhat from that of some other writers in the field, who mean by it a general emotional or attitudinal "tone" which exists throughout the organization. The characteristics denoted in the present usage are not feelings but practices, and they are somewhat different from one group to another within the organization. Each group exists within a climate that is somewhat unique to its particular point in the space that is the organization. Groups within the same department will experience slight differences among themselves in organizational climate. Much greater differences will exist among groups who come from different departments or who are at different levels in the organization, and very great differences will occur for groups drawn from different organizations.

A group which existed in a free space, subject to no external constraints, would be entirely free to do whatever it pleased. In fact, however, this seldom, if ever, occurs; the only occasion in which one might conceive its happening is during a period of general societal breakdown. Even if nothing else constrains, society—its laws and its government—places certain limits on what groups may and may not do. In formal organizations these constraints are considerable, and they increase in both number and intensity as one moves down the hierarchy. The board of directors has more latitude generally than do the president and his vice-presidents. The latter group has greater freedom than does any single vice-president with his division heads. Division heads have less latitude in working with their subordinate department heads than their superiors have in working with them, and so forth down to the lowest rung of the organizational ladder. These decreases in latitude are caused by the fact that objectives become set, policies determined, and standard practices instituted at higher echelons, to be applied principally to the operations of lower echelons. Objectives, policies, decisions, and directives are the end results of upper echelon groups (in fact, of all groups above the bottom level), and it is these results, for good or ill, which comprise organizational climate. It is perhaps best visualized as an accumulating wave, which rolls down through the organization, gaining some constraining power as it moves, in most instances increasingly constricting the latitude of the more subordinate groups which it envelops.

Managerial behavior, the other major causal area for events within any focal group, is determined in part by this climate of organizational conditions. Policies which prohibit or discourage the holding of group meetings, for example, have a profound, and detrimental, effect upon a subordinate manager's ability to employ group methods of supervision. He can also scarcely maintain high standards of performance against objectives that are inherently unreasonable, unattainable, or unclear. In part his behavior is also determined by factors specific to him as a person, such as the information which he has acquired over time about what is effective or appropriate (included in this category are his perceptions and expectations), his skills in actually engaging in a particular form of behavior, and his values. In most situations, these several sources make separate inputs to his behavior, and the result is some combination of their thrusts. It should be emphasized, however, that each is a separately limiting factor: this is especially true of organizational climate. For example, a manager with great skill, who is well informed, and who sincerely values doing an effective job can do nothing of the kind if the climate prohibits or prevents it. Neither information inputs, confronting the effects of his values, nor all the skill training in the world will make any impact in such a situation until that climate changes so as to permit him to behave differently.

Somewhat subsequent to these two causal factors of organizational climate and managerial behavior, yet antecedent to intervening processes per se, is the behavior of peer subordinates toward one another. Their behavior can be described according to the same dimensions as that of the manager: within their peer group they are to some degree supportive in their behavior toward one another, or they are not; they maintain high standards of performance in ways which spread a contagious enthusiasm, or they do not; they make certain that their particular information and technical know-how is available to one another, or they withhold it; and they encourage close ties with one another, or they discourage them. Like the manager's behavior, the behavior of his subordinates is in part caused by the organizational climate in which they all live, and in part by their information, perceptions, expectations, skills, and values. In part, however, their behavior is caused by the manager's own behavior, either as a reflection of the way in which he deals with him, or as a reaction to it. His supportive example, as it grows, leads to increased supportiveness in their dealings with one another. As he becomes less supportive and more punitive, however, he will very likely stimulate in them pernicious rivalries, destructive competition, and efforts to maintain his favor, even if it is at the expense of their fellow members. This reflective process has a bottom limit, of course; at some point they will become more, not less, supportive of one another in response to his punitive behavior, as a measure of mutual defense against a shared threat.

From these causal and semicausal events the basic processes of the group are formed. The group has an effective flow of information within it because these events have been constructive, or it lacks that flow because they have not. It makes decisions well or poorly, coordinates its efforts adequately or inadequately, sufficiently influences events to prevent errors and slippage or allows them to be determined by happenstance, and is motivated to perform or is not.

Between these intervening group processes and hard performance results is a class of outcomes that is partly intervening in nature, partly results in its own right. These outcomes are measures of health, satisfaction, and "personnel performance" (such as manpower turnover, grievance rate, absence rate, and the like). Poor employee health, low satisfaction, high turnover and excessive absence are "intervening" in the sense that they are costly to the organization, representing lost product and/or high operating costs. They are end results as well, since they represent human costs which, if not paid by the organization directly, are paid by it indirectly as society asks it to shoulder its share of the load of repairing the human damage which results. Often the cost to the organization is highly visible, as in those instances, apparently on the rise currently, in which a disgruntled, carefully anonymous employee tosses a tool, such as a wrench or hammer, over his shoulder into the conveyor mechanism. It is illustrated even more pointedly in a case the writer has encountered, an important managership which only one person has managed in recent years to hold and live. By "live" is not meant organizational survival; it is meant in a literal, physical sense. All

but one have "died with their boots on," from such conditions as cardiovascular disease aggravated, one presumes, by
the stress, conflict, and pressure which the position entails!

End results are far more familiar. At the lowest hierarchical levels they consist of output rate, operating costs, quality
of product or service, and, ultimately, earnings. At upper hierarchical levels they consist of the intangible product of the
group's efforts, in the form of policy statements or interpre-
tations, basic objectives, decisions, and directives. The sheer
number of these intangible products which an upper level
group turns out in a given period of time is perhaps intrinsi-
cally important, as is the amount of resources which they
consume in doing so. Quality is perhaps more important,
however, since their product permeates the life of large seg-
ments of the entire organization.

The flow of events is not only from one set of characteristics to another within a group, however; it is also, as stated
earlier, from one level of the organization to another.

The effects of a condition at the top management level
are traced through the rest of the organization in figure 2. In
this simple case, the top manager has decided for reasons of
his own not to employ group methods of supervision. His
subordinates, therefore, have little or no opportunity to discuss issues of general impact with one another in a group setting, and matters are instead handled on a one-by-one basis
by each of them with the manager alone. The frame of reference becomes the welfare of that particular department, or
perhaps of one or two other departments where the potential
impact is readily recognizable. More obscure side effects,
many of them of serious proportions, will slip by unhandled,
however, and coordination among the major departments will
to some degree suffer.

This decrement in coordination becomes an organizational climate problem for groups at the upper-middle management level. Because operations are less coordinated than

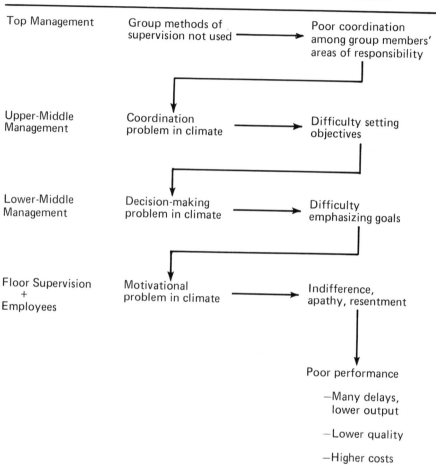

	CONDITION	RESULT
Top Management	Group methods of supervision not used	Poor coordination among group members' areas of responsibility
Upper-Middle Management	Coordination problem in climate	Difficulty setting objectives
Lower-Middle Management	Decision-making problem in climate	Difficulty emphasizing goals
Floor Supervision + Employees	Motivational problem in climate	Indifference, apathy, resentment

Poor performance

—Many delays, lower output

—Lower quality

—Higher costs

Fig. 2. A HYPOTHETICAL FLOW OF CLIMATE AND GROUP EVENTS DOWN THE HIERARCHY

they might be, groups at this level have trouble setting objectives that are meaningful. In operations that are interdependent it is often found that objectives are mutually contradictory. Objectives are sometimes no sooner set and disseminated than they are superseded by a shift in priorities stemming from an attempt to resolve the coordination dilemma by those at the level above. The net result is ambiguity and confusion, which appears to those in lower-middle management as a decision-making climate problem. To groups at this level, decisions appear to be based upon something other than complete information, contain obvious absurdities, are often unclear and contradictory, or are perhaps incomplete. For group members at this level, this lack of clarity in the decision-making structure of the climate creates great difficulty in setting high performance goals. What the situational performance requirements are is quite unclear, and it may be difficult to distinguish what is not high enough from that which is too high (or simply off target entirely). Thus we may find groups at this level stressing output level at the expense, if necessary, of quality, when, in fact, the organization's real requirement is precisely the opposite. Or one group, early in the production process, may emphasize lowering costs at the expense of additional volume, when another group, later in the process, has geared itself operationally and attitudinally for a high volume push.

At the lowest level of the organization (the floor supervisor and his employees) this creates a motivational climate which discourages, rather than encourages, effective accomplishment. The organization appears not to know what it is doing, and an enthusiastic commitment to one course of attainment, carefully built up by a process of involvement, is soon aborted by shifting signals from above. It takes very few such occurrences to "turn off" the nonsupervisory employees. They very rapidly learn not to plunge enthusiastically into anything, since it very likely will be meaningless in a short time. The result is indifference, apathy, and resentment, and the outcome for the organization is poorer performance caused by a great many delays, lower quality, and higher costs. The organization, therefore, pays heavily by a process of compounded error for the reluctance of its top manager to use group methods of supervision. The tragedy is not simply that it has happened, but that the real cause is not likely to be known or understood, and that the blame will likely be laid at the doorstep of those much farther down in the hierarchy, who are themselves largely hapless victims.

Lag Time

In the flow of events through groups and down through the hierarchy, instantaneousness is not a fact of life. An expansion of the illustration just given may serve to explain this. Let us assume that the top manager suddenly comes to realize the true situation confronting his organization and that he concludes he can remedy it by shifting his own style of working to a group method of supervision. He calls a group meeting of his subordinates, explains the problem as he understands it, and announces that he now proposes to conduct most of their work within a group framework. Regardless of his saying that he wants them henceforth to pull together in solving this and other problems in a group setting, they will, almost to a man, continue behaving in their customary manner of rivalries and one-upmanship and will still attempt to gain his ear privately. This will occur, not because of any inherently "diabolical" streak in their natures, but for a few very simple reasons. For one thing, they are accustomed to a very different behavior pattern on his part, and they will likely view his initial attempts either with suspicion (i.e., what is the sly old fox up to?) or as a passing whim.

If he persists, however, and confronts his subordinates

with the effects of their behavior and his own, on a second or third (or sixth or eighth) attempt, one or two members may in fact give his new method a try. The remainder will still not believe that anything is, in the long run, any different. Several attempts later, a third or fourth member may become aware of the difference and join the first two. It may be weeks or months before enough group members are aboard to reach some "critical mass" necessary to make an impact on their functioning as a group.

Because they are unaccustomed to this new group format, their efforts are likely to be clumsy for awhile, and it will take a period of time before they are, as a group, experiencing sufficiently improved coordination to (a) make any difference and (b) become noticed by those upper-middle management groups subordinate to them.

With coordination, which has up to this time been a limiting factor, now improved, upper-middle management groups can now set clearer, more realistic objectives. But will they? Not immediately: for one thing, they have not had to do so before, and it is likely to be a bit unnerving to them to assume clear responsibility where the excuse of ambiguity has been a way of life. Even if they attempt it, however, they are likely to falter a bit at first. Here, again, a period of time will be required before (a) an amount of improvement of any size has been achieved, and (b) this improvement becomes noticed by lower-middle management groups.

With better objective setting by groups immediately above them, the decision-making climate improves for lower-middle management. They are in theory now able to do a better job of emphasizing high performance goals. They are not likely to show rapid gains in this area, however. This is a skill that takes both practice and polish, and time is once more required to (a) gain the skill and (b) make the gain large enough to be both noticed and convincing.

Only as the last link, an improved motivational climate,

is put into place, will indifference, apathy, and resentment begin to abate. Once more, it will require a period of time, of careful, hesitant trials at feeling a little different about things, before this change occurs in any appreciable magnitude. It will require some time beyond this—at least until the end of the next accounting period—for results to be shown in performance.

When we consider all of these consecutive events, in terms of the frequency of opportunities to try something different and the number of trials necessary to develop and to convince, it becomes obvious that we are talking about a period of months, or perhaps years, for a major change at the top to trickle down to the bottom of the organization.

The top manager reading this account of a rather sluggish natural flow of events down through an organization may feel that the description does not square with his experience. He may feel that he has a greater capacity to make things happen *immediately* than our illustration implies.

In part this is an illusion. Persons in the organizational stratosphere, because they cannot be simultaneously at all points where a directive must be implemented, mistake the issuing of a directive for its fulfillment in fact. They also mistake the flurry of activity which their presence stimulates for compliance with their wishes. If, in fact, a top manager could watch on videotape his progress through an organization on a typical day, he would probably see a crescendo of scurrying and words that rises as he approaches a particular location (or as it approaches him), reaches an apex in his presence, and diminishes as he fades into the distance.

In part, however, his capacity for direct impingement is greater than our previous illustration suggests. In many ways he does move directly in on the lowest levels of the organization, often in response to data appearing in the operating reports provided by staff units. These data are, of course, portraits of events already over and done with; nothing he now

does can reverse them. He assumes, however, that, all other
things being equal, the most accurate prediction about events
tomorrow is the course they have followed in the period immediately preceding. When things have been going well,
therefore, he usually abstains from interfering; when the data
show that all has not gone well, he intervenes. Often his inter-
ventions take such forms as across-the-board budget cuts and
manning reductions, directives to get performance up *or else*
(where "or else" means discharge or demotion), or tinkering
with the piece rate structure.

Each of these direct impingements, however, requires
continuous surveillance by persons or agencies seldom on the
site continuously. Even then, each contains a built-in tendency
to be self-defeating. Arbitrary budget cuts lead to padding
in anticipation of future budget cuts. "Or else" pressures
lead some group members to self-select out of the system;
when that happens, it is not the poorer performers who leave.
Rather, it is the better trained, more highly skilled members
who leave, because it is they who receive other employment
offers and who realize that they need not endure an organizational life of unreasonable pressure. Piece-rate tinkering leads
to slowdowns, sabotage, and a piling up of grievances at contract negotiation time. The response, of course, is to build in
surveillance mechanisms, additional persons and agencies
whose task it is to watch the results of the surveillance agencies already established. Each effort to outlaw undesirable results produces a further undesirable reaction, which requires
still more surveillance apparatus, and what began as a problem involving a few persons gradually expands into the same,
but bigger, problem studied by a large, highly paid staff.

What the top manager does in this instance is to short-
circuit the system. It is, in many ways, similar to putting a
penny in the fuse socket: the power will flow, the light will
work, but the system may overload and destroy itself in the
process. Nor is it at all obvious that he can short-circuit the

system in a positive way; instead, his possibilities in this area appear to be limited to the negative aspect. He can coerce and pressure for certain outcomes directly upon the lowest levels of the organization, but he cannot provide positive, adaptive capability without himself doing all of those things which are at present not done. If, for example, he were super-human enough to be able personally and effectively to stimulate an enthusiasm for one hundred different sets of goals within one hundred different work groups, he might alleviate the motivational climate problem in our early illustration. Obviously he cannot. He can only build in the necessary degree of adaptability and capacity for effective functioning by creating in his own immediate subgroup those conditions which in turn will create other conditions that will ultimately create the desired state of affairs.

Some amount of lag time, therefore, is a simple fact of organizational life. Its length in any particular setting depends upon a great number of factors, including at least the nature of the specific problems and conditions at various levels of the organization, the backgrounds, beliefs, values, and skills of those persons in positions at those levels, the length of time during which present conditions have existed, and the nature of the task or technology involved.

If lag time is, as we have suggested, in part a problem of the period required for behavioral events to move noticeably through the system, it is also in part a problem of the kinds of whole-organization characteristics which change more and less quickly. Attitudes ordinarily change prior to a change in absence or turnover rate. Productivity, costs, and waste change somewhat more slowly. Labor relations, negotiations difficulties, and substantial shifts in the grievance rate take a bit more time. Quality of product suffers later, and customers abandon the product or service only after their experience tells them that it is no longer up to the standard which it once met. One may disagree with the order in which these are presented as occurring, but the point remains: different outcomes change at different times. Those early in the sequence affect those coming later. Depending upon which outcomes one is focusing on, lag time may be greater or less.

The Systemic Character of the Organization

The preceding discussion serves to explain why it is that one cannot, in any serious attempt to understand and manage an organization, safely ignore the social and psychological structure of that organization. Events interrelate selectively. Not all aspects of organizational climate affect all behaviors within the group; even those which affect the same behaviors affect them at different rates and different points. Not all behaviors combine in the same way to produce all outcomes for the group. Furthermore, outputs stemming from the process of one group become structural inputs of a particular kind for other groups.

This leads us to what must by now be an obvious point: that the various behavioral, attitudinal, and structural parts of the organizational whole have a fundamental interdependence, and that they must be mutually consistent. We have observed in our well-worked illustration what might conceivably happen if a top manager were to ignore only one aspect of effective organizational management, the use of group methods of supervision. Other, different illustrations could be given as well. The point is that one cannot graft parts of one management system onto parts of another and have any meaningful whole. One cannot, for example, attach a participative decision-making system to an autocratic communication system, since the mistrust, hostility, and inaccuracy of the latter will rapidly destroy the former. One cannot attach an emphasis upon high performance goals to a system lacking supportive behavior and expect the result to be anything except an increase in unreasonable pressure and resistance. One cannot profitably attach high technical competence to a communication system which chronically mistrusts all messages.

It is not that it is inadvisable to attempt these mismatched combinations; it is simply that it cannot be effectively done. The system will gravitate toward an integrity in one kind of system or another. Where an attempt is made artificially to implant intervening or lower echelon processes of a participative nature in an organization in which causal or upper echelon processes are more autocratic, it is likely that the whole system will shift, or revert, toward autocracy. Where implantation of participative *causal* practices is attempted, it is more likely that the system will move in that direction. This is closely tied to the whole question of organizational change and development, which will be discussed in greater depth in a subsequent chapter. For the present it is sufficient simply to underscore the basic integrity of the system.

Systems 1 to 4: Increments of Effective Functioning

Likert has described the general properties of highly organized management systems in terms of a continuum ranging from those systems which are most autocratic to those systems which are most participative. Although the dimension described is, in fact, continuous, and any particular organization might fall at any spot on it, Likert has identified four generally distinguishable areas of the continuum and presented capsule descriptions of them. Most autocratic is System 1, labeled "Exploitive Authoritative." This system hoards control and direction at the very top of the organization, decisions are made at the very top, orders are issued. Although there is some downward communication, and, in fact, a great deal of effort may be expended attempting to communicate

accurately downward, these communications are perceived
with hesitancy and suspicion by subordinates. On too many
occasions they have found themselves burned by trusting too
literally what a superior says. There is, however, very little
upward communication and little or no lateral communication. As a result, the decisions which are made at the top of
the organization are based upon partial information, which is
often inaccurate. In System 1 organizations, as in all organizations, control data are necessary and present, but in System 1 these data are often distorted and falsified by subordinates in an effort at self-protection. Since there is no effort
built in to develop that natural motivation which involvement produces, the organization instead relies upon fear,
upon the need for money, and upon a desire for status or
power, ignoring other motives which are intrinsic to the person or inherent in groups. These motives, of course, do not
disappear; they remain present and have their effect. Their effect, however, is ordinarily contrary to the organization's interest, and so the motivational force pattern in System 1 is
largely one of mutual cancellation: certain motives cancel
out, rather than reinforce, other motives. Mistrust is prevalent, and an informal organization, contrary to the formal organization's needs, develops, stimulating covert resistance to
the orders which were perhaps verbally agreed to and accepted.
Not only mistrust but hostility and dissatisfaction are present
in the organization. There is little motivation to fulfill the organization's tasks and only those at the very top of the organization feel responsibility for the organization's success. Although the top managers may feel that they have a great deal
of control, their position in a complex organization in a democratic society is more nearly like that of the one-eyed man
in the kingdom of the blind. What control exists, they have,
but the total is precious little.

System 2, labeled "Benevolent Authoritative," improves
somewhat upon System 1. Not all decisions are made at the

very top of the organization. Policy is decided at the top, but specific implementation decisions may be delegated to somewhat lower levels. Orders are still issued, but some opportunity may well be provided for subordinate individuals to comment upon those orders. There is a great deal of downward communication, viewed ordinarily with mixed feelings by subordinates. There is very little upward communication, much of it distorted and filtered, and practically no lateral communication. Fear is less a motivational force in System 2 than it is in System 1, although here it is also used occasionally. System 2 relies instead more heavily upon the need for money, desire for status, and other allied individual ego motives. The untapped motives still exist, as they did in System 1, and still in some measure cancel out those motivational forces relied upon by the organization. Attitudes are sometimes hostile, sometimes favorable, but there is ordinarily a substantial degree of dissatisfaction present in the organization, and although managers usually feel responsible for the organization's well-being, the rank and file membership usually does not. As in System 1, an informal organization often exists, parallel to the formal and working contrary to the formal organization's interests. Real control, therefore, is usually less than that presumed to exist by management personnel.

System 3, termed "Consultative," improves in its turn upon System 2. Here, broad policy only is determined at the top. More specific decisions are made at lower levels. The information upon which they are based is reasonably accurate and adequate. Some use is made of group decision-making processes, and to the extent that this is true a contribution is generated from decision making to motivation. Practically no reliance is placed upon fear or coercion, and use is made of most major motive sources inherent in the individual—the need for money, ego motives, and the desire for new experience. Little use is made, however, of those motivational forces inherent in group process. Goals are set, or orders are

SYSTEM 1: EXPLOITIVE AUTHORITATIVE

Motivational Forces	Communication Pattern
Taps fear, need for money, and status. Ignores other motives, which cancel out those tapped. Attitudes are hostile, subservient upward, contemptuous downward. Mistrust prevalent. Little feeling of responsibility except at high levels. Dissatisfaction with job, peers, supervisor, and organization.	Little upward communication. Little lateral communication. Some downward communication, viewed with suspicion by subordinates. Much distortion and deception.

Interaction-Influence Process	Decision-Making Process
No cooperative teamwork, little mutual influence. Little upward influence. Only moderate downward influence, usually overestimated.	Decisions made at top, based upon partial and inaccurate information. Contributes little motivational value. Made on man-to-man basis, discouraging teamwork.

Goal-Setting Process	Control Process
Orders issued. Overt acceptance. Covert resistance.	Control at top only. Control data often distorted and falsified. Informal organization exists, which works counter to the formal, reducing real control.

SYSTEM 2: BENEVOLENT AUTHORITATIVE

Motivational Forces	Communication Pattern
Taps need for money, ego motives such as desire for status and for power, sometimes fear. Untapped motives often cancel out those tapped, sometimes reinforce them. Attitudes are sometimes hostile, sometimes favorable toward organization, subservient upward, condescending downward, competitively hostile toward peers. Managers usually feel responsible for attaining goals, but rank and file do not. Dissatisfaction to moderate satisfaction with job, peers, supervisor, and organization.	Little upward communication. Little lateral communication. Great deal of downward communication, viewed with mixed feelings by subordinates. Some distortion and filtering.

Interaction-Influence Process	Decision-Making Process
Very little cooperative teamwork, little upward influence except by informal means. Moderate downward influence.	Policy decided at top, some implementation decisions made at lower levels, based on moderately accurate and adequate information. Contributes little motivational value. Made largely on man-to-man basis, discouraging teamwork.

Goal-Setting Process	Control Process
Orders issued, perhaps with some chance to comment. Overt acceptance, but often covert resistance.	Control largely at top. Control data often incomplete and inaccurate. Informal organization usually exists, working counter to the formal, partially reducing real control.

SYSTEM 3: CONSULTATIVE

Motivational Forces

Taps need for money, ego motives, and other major motives within the individual. Motivational forces usually reinforce each other. Attitudes usually favorable. Most persons feel responsible. Moderately high satisfaction with job, peers, supervisor, and organization.

Communication Pattern

Upward and downward communication is usually good. Lateral communication is fair to good. Slight tendency to filter or distort.

Interaction-Influence Process

Moderate amount of cooperative teamwork. Moderate upward influence. Moderate to substantial downward influence.

Decision-Making Process

Broad policy decided at top, more specific decisions made at lower levels, based upon reasonably accurate and adequate information. Some contribution to motivation. Some group-based decision making.

Goal-Setting Process

Goals are set or orders issued after discussion with subordinates. Usually acceptance both overtly and covertly, but some occasional covert resistance.

Control Process

Control primarily at top, but some delegation to lower levels. Informal organization may exist and partially resist formal organization, partially reducing real control.

SYSTEM 4: PARTICIPATIVE GROUP

Motivational Forces

Taps all major motives except fear, including motivational forces coming from group processes. Motivational forces reinforce one another. Attitudes quite favorable. Trust prevalent. Persons at all levels feel quite responsible. Relatively high satisfaction throughout.

Communication Pattern

Information flows freely and accurately in all directions. Practically no forces to distort or filter.

Interaction-Influence Process

A great deal of cooperative teamwork. Substantial real influence upward, downward, and laterally.

Decision-Making Process

Decision making done throughout the organization, linked by overlapping groups, and based upon full and accurate information. Made largely on group basis, encouraging teamwork.

Goal-Setting Process

Goals established by group participation, except in emergencies. Full goal acceptance, both overtly and covertly.

Control Process

Widespread real and felt responsibility for control function. Informal and formal organizations are identical, with no reduction in real control.

Fig. 3. DESCRIPTIONS OF MANAGEMENT SYSTEM PROPERTIES

issued after discussion with subordinates, and in this sense, there is a distinct improvement in System 3 over System 2. Attitudes are, therefore, usually favorable; there is very little hostility, most persons in the organization do feel a responsibility for its welfare, and resistance to the organization's directives is at a low level. An informal organization may, to some degree, still exist, and to the extent it does, dilutes the real control available to the formal organization.

System 4, the most democratic on the continuum, is termed the "Participative Group" system. In this system, decisions are made throughout the organization and are linked together by the existence of overlapping groups which do the decision making. Goals are established by group participation, except in emergencies, and for this reason are fully accepted, both overtly and covertly. Information flows freely upward, downward, and laterally, and there exist practically no forces to distort or filter that information. System 4 taps all of the major positive motives, including those motivational forces which arise from group processes. No use is made of fear or coercion, and as a result, attitudes are quite favorable. The interpersonal climate is one of trust. The formal and informal organizations are identical. For these reasons, there exists no subrosa organization working contrary to the organization's purposes.

It must be obvious from the description just provided and from the material presented in figure 3 that strong terms are used to describe these four management systems. Having presented them in this way, it is important that we acknowledge that no top management group in its right mind would consciously describe itself in those terms used with reference to System 1. All would perhaps like to think of themselves as employing methods identifiable with System 4. This is understandable, because the fear which System 1 generates is pointedly not experienced by the top managers who create that system; rather, it accrues to subordinate members. The statement that the description begs the outcome, that no one would knowingly select System 1 or System 2 as his preferred method of working is an inadequate explanation of the results. Managers do elect by their behavior to implement System 2, if not System 1. System 2 with all of its inherent difficulties is perhaps the most prevalent management system in American industry today.

The general pattern of research findings has been that the closer an organization's management system is to System 4, the more effective is that organization in those terms which it itself values: lower costs, higher productivity, lower absence rate, and the like. Conversely, the closer an organization is to System 1, the less effective it is in those same terms. In addition, as an organization by purposeful development efforts moves from System 1 or System 2 to a position in System 3 or System 4, its productivity improves. If this is the case, it perhaps seems strange that organizations do not elect to move en masse toward the System 4 end of the continuum. That they obviously do not and have not has at least one of its causes in the measurement processes which they employ. This is the topic which the subsequent chapter will discuss in some depth.

A caution should be added as a final note to this discussion of Likert's four systems. In his writings to date he has described System 4 as the most effective pattern of management currently in use in American business. Few organizations have actually obtained it thus far. Far more may be found at System 2 or System 3 on the continuum. If there is a current trend, it may well be toward System 2 rather than away from it, even though societal forces now building appear to press urgently toward the System 4 model. That the dimension ends at present at System 4 is indicative of nothing except the current state of knowledge. Likert in no way conceptualizes System 4 as the ultimate form of organization. It is not a "best" model since others may lie beyond it.

There may well be a System 5, or a System 6. If there are these additional systems, their characteristics await further research and theory building.

Management as a Generalizable Process

Much has been made by other writers of what at first reading appears to be an eminently reasonable assumption, that different situations call for different management systems. This is a view which Likert in his writings has not concurred with; rather his view is that management is the same process wherever found, that the same basic principles operate in all instances. Management according to this conceptualization contains universal and transferable properties. He identifies at least three basic reasons why this is true.

1. Human nature basically, and in terms of inherited qualities, is the same the world over.
2. The scientific method is the same in all nations.
3. Culture may influence the method of application of basic principles of management, but culture is not itself a basic principle of management.

As the scientific method is applied, therefore, to the problem of management in different cultures and different settings in the world, it is likely that, because the same ingredients are involved, efforts will arrive at the same principles. With increasing industrialization, cultural differences will very likely diminish. For one thing, industrialization creates large-scale enterprises with large numbers of employees and with substantial interdependence. One important by-product of this is an increase in urban living and a decrease in that village life where cultural differences are most prevalent. Also the technologies of a given industry tend to be the same everywhere, as do the sociotechnical systems created to operate industrial plants. Finally, the differences that exist from industry to industry, technology to technology, or setting to setting, have not so much to do with the basic principles of management that exist but with the manner in which these principles are implemented in any given setting, and with the lag time described above. The greater length of time required in certain settings for end results to flow from the functioning of the system and differences in specific actions are variables which do not change the appropriateness of basic system principles and characteristics.

CHAPTER 9

Measuring
Human Resources

Many characteristics distinguish the modern industrial society from its medieval and more primitive forebears, not the least of which is its tendency to measure more things with greater accuracy. In some of the most central areas of our lives, those things which we consume, use, and do, substantial increases have taken place even within the last seventy-five years in the extent to which accurate measurement occurs. Whereas firewood cleared from one's own property once found its way to the fireplace or the kitchen range simply as needed, electricity, gas, or oil is now metered and billed to fill those same needs. Our clothing was once scrubbed by hand on a washboard, then boiled, until in the judgment of the housewife it was clean; it is now washed, rinsed, and dried automatically at temperatures and for lengths of time that are preset with relative precision. Water, instead of being dipped from creek,

well, or spring at whatever hazard that entailed and in quanti-
ties estimated to be sufficient, is now delivered to the use
point in measured volumes, and in most instances following a
periodic bateria count. Building materials and clothing are
manufactured in standard sizes; the nutrients in the food we
eat can be, and often are, calculated for us and listed on the
package. The tools we use have rated capacities; our medi-
cines are calculated in dosage units. Censuses describe the
properties of the whole nation. The smallest city lot is laid
out by the surveyor, and we receive traffic tickets and fines
for measured speeds in excess of a predetermined limit.

This is, of course, no mere aberration of our age, despite
the reaction of some who feel that mankind is becoming
"stapled, folded, spindled, and mutilated" in the interest of
impersonal numbering systems. Quantification permits rapid
calculations about whole classes of objects and events, and as
a result actions can be taken quickly and with some assurance
that they will be appropriate. Making use of its most recent,
perhaps most glamorous extension, the electronic computer,
quantification permits complex judgments to be made more
rapidly. The result of all of this is the wide variety of auto-
matic tools and machines which enable man to accomplish a
great deal with a minimal effort. The town blacksmith could
shoe a horse with sufficient accuracy and speed to satisfy
both man and his beast; he could scarcely, by eyeball estimate, build components for an internal combustion engine
that would actually operate. Without an ability to manufac-
ture parts to closely measured tolerances, man would still be
on horseback.

Just as measuring distances in terms of time or "moons"
required for a man to walk them may have met the need of
the primitive man who seldom traveled, but hardly suffices
for modern interstate highway system maps, so describing a
management as "good," a manager as "competent," or attitudes as "positive" is inadequate to the task facing modern

organizations. Their behaviors and functional properties should be quantified for those same reasons which have promoted and sustained the development of measurement in other fields.

An effort in this direction did, of course, begin in the 1930s. During the period since World War II, the initial trickle of organizational research has become a tidal wave, and yet an astute observer would note that the conclusions reached in the various studies scarcely appear to be consistent. Some studies have produced positive relationships, others negative ones, and still others no relationships at all between measures of the behavior and attitudes of managers and their subordinates on the one hand and performance on the other. Where, for example, one study has measured what it presumes to represent supportive behavior by a supervisor and found it positively related to cost performance, another may well have found similar measures to be negatively related. Looking at this confusing array, a few reviewers concluded several years ago that there may well be no dependable, reliable association between these two areas.

More recent evidence suggests, however, that these contradictions may be the result of the methods used in the different studies, not a reflection of what goes on in the real world. For one thing, measures used by various investigators have differed both in quality and in kind. A questionnaire item dashed together hurriedly to meet a reporting deadline and phrased in words which happen to have struck the investigators's fancy may well measure something far different from what it is proposed to tap. In addition, similarities may be assumed where none is warranted: one researcher may have studied manager self-descriptions in relation to manpower turnover in that manager's immediate group, whereas another, whose study is commonly thought to have been looking at the same problem area, may instead have related descriptions by a manager's superior to absence rate for the described man's entire department. If the results are found to be consistent, a reviewer may propose a general principle; if they are inconsistent, he may conclude that no real pattern exists. Whatever he concludes by way of common meaning, however, is likely to be unwarranted.

Although inexact comparisons and measures present a substantial problem, perhaps the most serious difficulty stems from the fact that many, if not most, of the studies have been single-time investigations. Information about managerial practices or subordinate attitudes has been collected once, e.g., during the third week of March, and then related to performance for that same time. Or performance for some period of months surrounding or following the time managerial behavior was measured has been collapsed into a single average reading, which has then been related in some way to the former.

In contrast to this, our discussion of lag time in the preceding chapter certainly suggests that any serious effort to understand organizational processes and their effects must consider a number of points in time, not merely a single instance. Studies must measure organizational characteristics on repeated occasions, and performance for a number of periods, before, during, and perhaps long afterward, to determine the real relationship which exists. In many ways the problem is analogous to a comparison between a single snapshot and a motion picture. Consider the following photograph: two men, one in white trunks and one in black, standing in similar positions facing one another, arms outstretched, with a basketball in midair between them. From this photo alone, an observer could not determine whether white had thrown the ball to black, or vice versa. But a number of pictures at spaced intervals, connected together, and projected on a screen soon makes it obvious which had in fact occurred.

It is precisely because today's performance is seldom, if ever, the product of today's management, but rather the product of management practices which occurred last week, last month, or last year, that many measurements, taken sequentially over time, must be obtained. An employee who has built up a record of chronic absenteeism as a way of temporarily escaping from a harsh supervisor is not absent on a particular Tuesday because of anything that happens on that Tuesday, but because of a piling-up of happenings over many months. To find the organizational or managerial behavior which first set in motion this chronic response, it might be necessary to have measured those practices fully a year or two before. Similarly, today's lagging output rate may be the persisting result of managerial decision making five or ten years prior to the date of its occurrence, and a present unfortunate pattern of labor relations may stem from behaviors which first began during the early 1940s!

For this reason—different outcomes which occur after different amounts of lag time—results can be confusing and contradictory. An investigator may have inadvertently chosen for collecting his data that particular point at which managerial behavior has begun to improve substantially in some units or departments but where attitudes have not yet changed as a result of it and where performance is still responding to yesterday's pressure artistry. If so, he will find that better interpersonal relations on the supervisor's part have absolutely no relationship to the attitudes of subordinates, and that they are *negatively* associated with performance. However, had he taken as his measure of outcomes those performance statistics which truly stem from the changes taking place, and those changed attitudes which really result from improved managerial behavior—those occurring several weeks or months later—his findings would probably have been consistently positive. The assumption, therefore, that there should be a simple correspondence at a single point in time is unwarranted. The relationships are far more complex than that simple assumption permits.

The lag time concept is tied to another problem which often arises to confound the interpretation of research results in this area. It stems from the way in which one determines what the true lag time is in any given situation. Often it occurs when a researcher poses to himself and to others a question similar to the following: is System 4 the best one to use in all situations, or is each of the four systems (1, 2, 3 and 4) "best" in some distinct setting? In an attempt to answer this question, the researcher may inadvertently allow a very slippery error to creep into his calculations. In an effort to obtain some criterion of what is "best" by way of outcomes, he may well simply go to top managers or officials of a number of different organizations and ask. Each response he receives, however, will contain some time perspective on the part of the manager himself: the measures he personally uses to determine quality of performance will take into account some period of time. If the manager happens to direct a research operation, his reponse may well indicate that he judges excellence on the basis of numbers of new developments or products turned out over a five-year period. If he happens to manage a production line, he may well give as his criterion adherence to the daily or weekly schedule or cost budget. If managers were all-seeing, the researcher would receive an accurate identification of what comprises the "best" in organizations. Unfortunately, they are likely to be human, fallible, and accepting of customary ways of viewing and judging things, and the investigator who accepts their responses may well become trapped in a distortion. Systems 1 and 2, composed as they are of hard, punitive pressure tactics, tend to produce splendid short-term results, with disastrous long-term consequences. Likert describes this situation in the following terms:

Let us look, for example, at a series of events which often take place in a department or plant engaged in an operation where performance standards and production schedules can be set. A man is put in charge of such a plant or department knowing that he will be favorably judged and rewarded if his department achieves a high level of production. He puts a good deal of pressure on his subordinates and pushes production up. Measurement of the end-result variables indicates that he is a "fine manager." In a year or two his reputation earns him a promotion to another department, where he repeats the performance. In the meantime, hostilities have been developing in his subordinates and those below them in the organization. Just about the time that he moves on, the results of his unreasonable pressure begin to show up in decreased loyalty in the organization, lack of motivation to do a job, turnover, slowdowns, and scrap loss. The new manager reaps the fruits of the promoted manager's behavior and gains the reputation of being a "poor manager," for almost as soon as he takes over, things begin to fall apart.[1]

If the reward and rotation policies combine in this way, as they often do, to produce an emphasis upon short-term gain, then our researcher will find that System 2 is more "appropriate" for short time-frame operations. In other organizations, such as research and development, where a product or innovation may be years in the development, a short-term focus is impossible, and a long-term perspective is necessarily taken, with performance measured accordingly. Quite naturally, one will conclude in this latter instance that System 4 is appropriate for research organizations. And the overall conclusion will be that one kind of organization requires one kind of system. The investigator's conclusions, however, will be the product of his own methodology: it is the lag time assumption which is erroneous, and it leads to false findings. True lag time must be estimated by measuring causes and results over a period of time, studying the waxing and waning of relationships, and locating that point at which the relationship is closest, the point at which it peaks.

Another issue in the lag time area creates occasional confusion. Likert, for example, has said,

> The optimum frequency for the measurements will vary with the kind of work involved. The more nearly the work involves the total man, such as research and development tasks, the shorter should be the intervals between successive measurements, for . . . the time lag between changes in the causal, intervening and end-result variables is much less for such work than for work which is machine-paced. . . . A scientist who feels resentful toward his organization or manager rapidly becomes unproductive. With machine-paced and similar work, which usually employs only a part of the capabilities of the total man, a longer period of time is required before the adverse effect of unfavorable reactions and attitudes manifest themselves in the forms of norms to restrict production. . . .[2]

Yet, in the preceding paragraph, research and development have been described as typically requiring a long-term focus. Are these inconsistent? Not at all: the point is that lag time includes two components, the time required for a change in organizational conditions to have an effect upon a man's job efforts, and the time required for a change in his job efforts to be visible in the operating records of the firm.

A senior scientist may become very rapidly disenchanted with capricious shifts in priorities or arbitrary slashes in his budget, precisely because his whole being is wrapped up in his work, yet the result of his disenchantment may not appear until one or two years later. Both elements of lag time are likely to be of longer duration in the case of the production worker, on the other hand, since it will take more time for the highly engineered, highly structured system in which he works to be affected by changes in organizational or managerial practices. In addition, because only a part of him is involved in his work, it will require a considerable accrual of negative events for this part of his life to become sufficiently overriding to result in a shift which will noticeably affect the production record.

To summarize, a great deal of effort has been devoted in recent years to measuring various aspects of human organizational life and their relationship to performance. The results have been less consistent than they should be because (a) researchers have often been, understandably, more concerned with a particular problem of professional interest to them than with comprehensive coverage of organizational functioning and (b) too little accurate attention has been paid to the fact of lag time in organizational life.

Measurement Needs of Human Organizations

Lag time is also lead time, however. If a manager has an accurate reading of causal events, and if he knows what intermediate and end results stem from those events, he can make mid-course corrections and thereby make a favorable outcome more likely. Consider, by way of analogy, an individual who proposes to travel from New York to San Francisco by automobile: he might, if he were foolish enough, simply jump into his car and head generally west, judging the success of his trip by whether the place at which he arrived at the ocean was or was not San Francisco. Of course, he may en route have taken an unfortunate turn, causing him to arrive instead at Key West, or perhaps Hudson Bay.

No modern day traveler is likely to follow a course as risky as this. He will, instead, observe highway signs, notice the names of communities through which he passes, and, comparing these to a road map, shift his course to arrive safely at his destination. Events in organizations are similarly a journey, and the wise manager should have in hand a reading of events likely to cause future outcomes. If, by obtaining periodic, accurate measurements of the supervisory practices, within-group relationships, and climate present in his organization he notices that a shift has occurred which is likely to be costly some months hence in the motivation and trust of employees, he can correct the situation before its negative impact is felt. He can similarly reinforce positive causal shifts whose ultimate effects have not yet been felt, but whose payoff potential is substantial. In this way the feedback cycle is shortened; the organization need not wait for ultimate success or costly failure to occur before judging whether corrective action is required.

An organization, therefore, should periodically collect, tabulate, and make available to its managers at all levels accurate measurements of the organizational climate, managerial leadership, peer group behavior, attitudes, and satisfactions existing within their respective areas of responsibility. The frequency with which this should be done depends, as we have already indicated, upon the lag time length within that organization, upon the presence of critical external events, or upon the existence of planned development programs. Organizations whose lag time is quite short, like those which are potentially subject to a strong buffeting from the market or the economy or those which are purposely attempting to improve their human organizational processes, should obtain measurements more frequently. Those which have long lag times and are comparatively insulated and stable need them less frequently. Thus frequency may vary; the need remains, however, and in fact, increases as organizations increase in size, complexity, and investment. A small retail shop can perhaps survive readily with informal soundings; but crude impressions become less accurate, more out of touch with reality, as size increases. In addition, the cost incurred in faulty decisions grows with the organization.

If it is important that these measurements be obtained on a regular basis, it is no less important that they be obtained carefully and with competence. As is the case with any other measurements, they will doubtless contain some margin of error, regardless of the degree of competence or skill of those doing the collecting and processing. Still, as Likert suggests,

> If there is any danger in using measurements of the preceding kind, it is not their lack of complete and absolute accuracy, it is that management will underestimate the skill required and assume that it is enough if a reasonably intelligent interviewer asks people questions, or if a questionnaire is made readily available. Such an attitude leads to costly mistakes and disillusionment with the whole measurement idea. In reality, the measurement of the variables just outlined is a complex process and requires competence in the social science field.[3]

Although the skeptic may feel that this suggests a perennial dependence upon a staff or consulting social scientist, nothing of the sort is intended. Once a measurement program is launched, and the organization is experienced in the use of its results, no professional assistance may be required. Until that point is reached, however, the professional help of social scientists with a high level of scientific competence in this methodology is required; it cannot be done by an untrained person.

Human Resources Accounting

Once the idea of lag time is accepted, and the alternative view that today's management produces today's results rejected, it follows that a manager or an organization makes an investment today, wisely or foolishly, for productive payoff to-

morrow or next year. It is as true in affairs of the human organization as it is in finance that an investment whose return
is not realized is a poor one. Firms invest sizable amounts of
money in recruiting, hiring, and training manpower. Management itself is an overhead expense undertaken in the anticipation that it will help guarantee productive results. Building a
large number of previously unacquainted individuals into a
network of overlapping teams, highly motivated and techni-
cally competent, requires a substantial outlay on the part of
the organization. Its cost is recovered, and a profit made, as
the efforts of these teams subsequently result in the production of goods and services sold in the market. One could
imagine an organization which makes a persistent practice of
purchasing the most up-to-date equipment, shouldering the
expense of installing and adjusting it, and then promptly dis-
mantling and disposing of it prior to any productive run.
What fantasy permits, stockholders will not, however, and
the management of such an organization would rather rapidly
be called to account. Yet many managements do precisely
that with the firm's human assets, and an accounting is seldom requested. Unreasonable pressure, arbitrary treatment,
and a generally punitive stance may well yield immediate,
perhaps even striking, increases in productivity. They also
produce hostilities, decreased loyalty, a lack of motivation to
do a good job, turnover, slowdowns, and scrap. Better personnel, who receive alternative offers, will leave in greater
numbers; output will be lost, or it may suffer in quality. Thus
it is not the present which suffers, but the future. The increase is obtained at a cost to the human assets of the organization, assets which are cashed in for a fraction of their
worth. The true meaning of this cannot be stressed too much:
it is not simply that recruiting and training money has been
lost and must be written off, or that managers have wasted
valuable supervisory time and effort; rather a credit which
the firm had carefully built up and stored for the future has

been squandered, and at discount rates! It is very much the same as if a responsible person had sold a portion of the plant at a cut rate and claimed the receipts as "profit." As Likert points out,

> Companies are very careful not to let managers of decentralized plants show spurious profits and earnings by juggling inventory or by failing to maintain plant and equipment. Their accounting procedures measure and report regularly on inventory and on the condition of plant and equipment. "Earnings" achieved by liquidating the assets represented in the human organization are just as spurious as those achieved by liquidating the investment in the plant.[4]

The reason for this goes to the root of classical assumptions about work and the firm. Organizational manpower has in the past often been viewed in somewhat the same terms as water and air. Thus our language contains terms such as "labor market" and "labor pool," which, accurate as they may be for certain gross economic purposes, inaccurately reinforce in the management's mind the notion of hands, to be hired and fired at will without repercussion, of time to be bought as needed and delivered when bought, and of minimal requirements from completely interchangeable persons. Human organizational outlays are treated as a cost, not as an investment, and no accounting of them as assets is given.

To paraphrase an old saying, what is out of mind is out of sight. Because we have not commonly thought in terms of the human assets of the firm, we have not attended to them in our accounting procedures. It is to the filling of this void that proposals about "human resources accounting" have been made. First mentioned by Likert more than fifteen years ago,[5] it has been expanded and developed by him and by others in the period since that time.[6] The term itself refers to procedures for attaching dollar estimates to the value of a firm's human organization and to its customer goodwill. An organization which loses capable, highly skilled personnel is worth less; one which gains such persons is worth more. Bickering, mistrust, hostility, and unresolvable conflict subtract from its worth, whereas the constructive use of differences of opinion, effective supervisory practices, and cooperative teamwork add to it.

Estimates of the value of an organization's human resources are difficult to obtain, primarily because the technology is new and the relationships among components not entirely worked out. For this reason, there is considerable virtue in developing such a system by alternative routes, since each route can serve as a check upon the accuracy of the others. To date, three routes or methods have been conceptualized; for convenience we may label them (*a*) the "Past Cost" method, (*b*) the "Start-up Cost" method, and (*c*) the "Future Payoff" method.

Using the "Past Cost" method, information would be retrieved from the firm's records about costs actually incurred in recruiting, hiring, and training persons currently with the organization. Although the total arrived at by adding together all such costs for each person in the company would probably be dazzlingly large, it would very likely still underestimate the true investment in the human organization. Unless it included some allowance for the costs of familiarization, it would not include in its calculation the investment made during that period when the members were establishing effective working relationships with one another.

The "Start-up Cost" procedure would turn our attention to an estimate of what it would cost, in the present market place and under current conditions, to build and bring up to present speed an organization identical to the one which now exists. (Whereas in investment terms, the first method would be more analogous to the purchase price of stock at the time we bought it, this present method is more akin to its current price on the exchange.)

Computing the value of the human organization by either of these first two methods, difficult though it may be, is a much simpler problem than that of estimating its value in terms of productive potential by the "Future Payoff" method. This third method requires that there be collected, frequently enough and for a long enough period to demonstrate the kind and magnitude of relationships across time, measurements of those organizational practices and characteristics described in the early part of the chapter. From a knowledge of causes, effects, and the time required for the former to lead to the latter, an ability is generated to predict, from an analysis of shifts in the causal variables, the likely course of future outcomes. A value to the organization at the present time of this future productive potential can then be calculated by a discounting procedure.

Although the suggestion that dollar values should be attached to the firm's human assets may at first glance appear to be a radical departure from accepted practice, and though the systematic efforts in this direction are still in their infancy, precedent already exists for it. Acquisition of one firm by another occurs in large numbers each year and, in each instance, requires the attachment of an appropriate value to the firm being purchased. The purchase price is ordinarily considerably higher than the sum of the current value of physical and financial holdings and reflects allowances both for customer goodwill and for the existence of a skilled, productive work force. The fact of this discrepancy indicates an inherent attachment to something resembling the value of human assets, but the calculation itself may well be faulty. Often it is based in large part upon the current and recent earnings record of the acquired firm. If it has been using an approach to cost reduction which relies upon arbitrary personnel limitations, across the board budget slashes, and unceasing pressure, it may well be at a point where earnings are high, but future potential is bleak. If so, an estimate based upon the "earnings" of the acquired firm will greatly inflate its true value.

Accounting for the value of a firm's human assets could, if it became accepted and customary practice, lead to the elimination of certain anomalies that presently exist. One of these is illustrated by Likert in an account which he gives of a discussion in which the value of a firm's human assets were estimated by a "Start-up Cost" procedure and compared to shareholders' equity.[7] In the illustration, the value of human assets which resulted from the estimate was $700 million; shareholders' equity was $500 million. A punitive cost reduction program, it is pointed out, could liquidate human assets to a fraction of their worth and add impressively to current "earnings." A 10 percent liquidation, sold at fifty cents on the dollar, would produce $35 million in spurious earnings, which, compared to the firm's actual previous year's earnings of $125 million, would appear to the unsuspecting to amount to a substantial increment in profitability. In fact, however, the "real" value of the holdings has been diminished; what the shareholders own is worth less than it formerly was. If not the stock, the value which they hold has been watered, as surely as if additional stock had been issued without value to cover it. As long as there is no quantitative measurement of the firm's human assets, its management can in this fashion obtain a sizable proportion of its earnings in any one year from their liquidation. That it happens all too frequently is less a sign of calculated malice than of simple ignorance: top managers, stockholders, and financial experts alike have lacked the information and the tools necessary to become aware of the effect of punitive cost reduction. In addition, accurate perception has been clouded by the fact that many cost reduction programs take place within a context of continuing technological innovation. New products are developed and introduced, operations are increasingly automated, and production processes improved as additional parts of an effort toward greater efficiency and success. These efforts generally have a marked effect on overall cost performance, and as a result tend to obscure the deterioration that the more pressure-oriented tactics are inducing. Likert states that,

> To further obscure events, many firms are able to achieve continuing cost improvement over a span of several years and, understandably, come to rely increasingly on staff innovators to overcome the growing resistance to change and improvement, rather than turning their attention equally to building a total organization oriented toward the optimal use of technological opportunities.[8]

Another anomaly has to do with the organization's response to environmental pressure. This is perhaps best illustrated by figure 4.

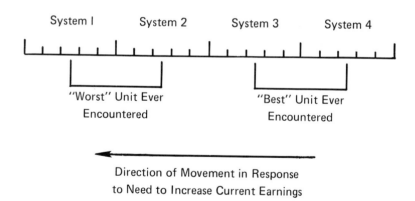

Fig. 4. SYSTEM DIFFERENCES AND RESPONSE TO
ENVIRONMENTAL PRESSURE

As this illustration shows, managers, when asked to describe the most efficient, effective organization or unit they have ever encountered, ordinarily place it well over toward System 4. Asked in similar fashion to describe the most inefficient, ineffective organization or unit which they have encountered, they place it far toward System 1 or Sytem 2. Managers were asked next to describe whether there exists any tendency for top management consciously to move in one direction or the other during those situations in which the press of environmental events is such that the organization needs every last ounce of current earnings that it can extract. Almost to a man, they agreed that it moves toward System 1 and away from System 4! In other words, at that very instant when it needs efficiency, it moves toward inefficiency; when it needs the dedicated efforts of all to survive a financial crisis, it consciously chooses a course likely to reduce chances of survival.

Several plausible reasons probably exist for what would otherwise seem to be a highly irrational course. For one thing, top managers feel threatened and apprehensive at such a turn of events in the environment, and they are less willing to trust subordinate levels to do the right thing. Trusting one's fate to others during difficult times is unnerving to most persons; to those accustomed to great organizational power it may well be overwhelming. In addition, there is often in such circumstances felt to be a need for immediate cash. More punitive stances, because they produce something tangible quickly, have more appeal. Today's problems are thus deferred until tomorrow, although that may be far from obvious to top managers currently weathering a storm.

In those anomalous situations, as in more normal operating states, the purpose of any system of human resources accounting is the same as that of obtaining quantitative measurements generally of the functional health and practices of the organization: its final usefulness is in providing information which may help the organization as a whole, and its management, make better decisions. Managers who lack information about the impact of what they do, both in the short and in the long runs, operate blindly. The more complete and accurate the information which they have about the resources entrusted to their stewardship, the more likely it is that the courses which they select will be wise ones. Careful attention to physical assets alone is not enough; reliance upon interpersonal openness alone, without rigorous measurement, is similarly insufficient. These are error-prone processes; given a sufficiently large number of cases, each of which is dealt with on organizational horseback, error will predominate.

CHAPTER 10

Implementing
System 4 Concepts

In this applications-minded age, no book about an organizational theory would be complete without a discussion of the implementation principles which the scholar allies with his concepts of form and function. Since the organizational concepts described in the preceding chapter were developed by locating those conditions which relate to organizational effectiveness, this becomes all the more necessary as a task for the present book, because enhancing effectiveness is a more urgent task than simply accounting for it. Although Likert's published statements may seem to be more concerned with description than implementation, it is not a correct conclusion that they contain no treatment of the applications problem. For one thing, the concepts spelled out as comprising System 4 contain an emphasis upon participation, high levels of interdependence and aspiration, accomplishment, and enhancement of personal worth. By their nature these are concepts of growth, development, and change. In addition, many of the concepts are stated in active, rather than simply abstract, terms. For example, in an early chapter of *New Patterns of Management*, the following phrasing is used: ". . . One of the ways the high-producing managers are achieving better communication and more accurate perceptions is by building greater peer-group loyalty."[1] Cause and effect are clearly implied in this statement; because a manager *does* something, something else changes in a desired direction. In this and similar ways, therefore, the material contained in a description of the System 1 to System 4 continuum is in part a theory of change as well as a theory of organizations.

More directly than this, however, specific ideas about application are found in Likert's writings from an early date, and in both *New Patterns of Management*[2] and *The Human Organization*[3] space is devoted specifically to a discussion of this issue. From a number of comments and remarks in sections of these books and in his earlier publications, at least a foretaste can be obtained of his views on organizational change, presumably to be reflected and elaborated in the future in a volume on this subject, mentioned as an intended product in the introductory chapter of his 1967 book.

Change as an Incremental Process

Constructive change is an adaptive process consisting of successive increments of movement occurring over a relatively long period of time; it is not a "conversion" experience which produces dramatic shifts in a matter of a few days or weeks. Those same aspects of lag time which affect our ability to understand accurately the relationships which exist between organizational climate, managerial behavior, group processes, and performance also affect our ability to change the organization in beneficial ways. If the appearance in the operating reports of figures demonstrating better performance is our criterion that something has changed or improved, then evidence of change will appear gradually, its speed depending upon the complexity of the organization and its technology, its "tallness" (i.e., how many layers of hierarchy change events must travel through), and the nature of the problems requiring change. The "first one, then another, then another" character of perceiving change and responding to it as believable almost guarantees that change will accumulate gradually, like bricks being stacked in a pile.

There is another reason why change tends to be, and must be, a gradual process of successive increments. It derives from the fact that there is a relatively close association between our values and our expectations on the one hand and our experiences on the other. This association is more than a simple coincidence of things commonly found together: there is a tendency for the one to flow from, or be caused by, the other. Although our values and expectations in part determine our behavior at any given moment, these personal characteristics, what we prize and what we anticipate, are more the product of our accumulating experiences than our experiences are the result of values and expectations. Our values and expectations change, therefore, as our experiences change. At any particular time, they set a limit of legitimacy or acceptability which applies to, and determines our reaction to, conditions which we experience. Change which is intended to be constructive and lasting can be no greater than this horizon of legitimacy permits. Movement toward participative practices, for example, can in any one period be no greater than our values hold to be acceptable. Change programs which attempt to put into place amounts and forms of participation greater than this limit are likely to produce not change, but fear and flight.[4] With greater experience of participation, however, will come an enlarged limit, and movement in the period which follows can then proceed beyond the old limit.[5]

Introducing a substantially different management system is likely to be a very large undertaking, more difficult in many ways than the introduction of a technological change of comparable size. Just as major technological changes are often introduced in a gradual, sequenced fashion over a period of two or three years to minimize dislocation and gain acceptance, so changes in the social or management system must be undertaken in careful, meaningfully sequenced increments that remain just within the boundary of acceptability and legitimacy.

Both the magnitude of the change required in toto and the size of the organization itself are related to the length of time necessary for change to occur and to the likelihood of a number of stepwise increments. The larger the total change required, and the larger the organization, the more likely it is that a change effort will require several years to be completed and that it will occur in a number of steps.

With this in mind, it is also better that, within the program plans for any increment, relatively modest targets be set. Particularly where the desire for change is great, but the sources of resistance strong, expectations which are set unrealistically high can result in disillusionment when real accomplishment, though substantial, is less than dramatic.[6]

Cooperation, Not Hostile Confrontation

Constructive change does not come from an angry, passionate collision of persons, but from the patient building of a structure of groups capable of cooperatively solving their problems. It requires that there be built bonds of interdependence, mutual influence, and trust.

Change programs which start from a position of, and rely heavily upon, hostile, emotional confrontation are basically coercive. Whether they consist of a top management which fixes blame, pounds tables, and demands that subordinate levels change in some direction which it happens to wish, or of subordinates or consultants who shout, threaten, embarrass, and disrupt, the result is likely to be that typical of coercion. As previous chapters have suggested, coercion and punitive surveillance produce compliance only as long as the coercive or surveillant agent remains active and within eyesight or earshot. The desired change will give evidence of existence only as long as that head of emotional steam and the threat of physical force behind it remain present. In the long run, coercion is likely to prove counter-productive as a change strategy, since those who were forced to adopt new ways will revert to old patterns. They may store up and feed upon their resentment and ultimately, at a time and in a way of their choosing, wreak double vengeance upon those who made life so unpleasant.

System 4 implies something more and better than this, however: it describes a set of practices and conditions which persist and succeed because they are positively viewed by the organization's members. This is, of course, not to say that hostility, aggression, counter-aggression, and emotionalism do not occur in the course of more positive change efforts (those allied to a System 4 framework). However, there is at least some reason to believe that the aggression which sometimes occurs in that circumstance is a ventilating *effect*, not a cause, of change. The real change has often already occurred, or at least begun, when the rank-and-file voice their pent-up resentments. As Likert describes it,

> Organizations operating under tight controls will have more difficulty in changing to the newer theory than will those companies whose present operations more nearly conform to it. The former not only will have to make greater changes in interactional processes and often in a

series of steps, but they are also likely to run into apathy, indifference and even aggressive responses. One might expect that any movement away from authoritarian control would be greatly appreciated by employees. Experience has shown, however, as have experiments that when a management relinquishes tight controls and moves toward participative management, the *initial* response of members of the organization at every hierarchical level may be apathy or open hostility and aggressive responses against their superiors. . . .[7]

Use of the Existing Authority Structure

It is precisely because purposeful change is a structured set of activities designed to alter the behavior and relationships of people in groups that change must occur from the "top down," not from the "bottom up." Within the work group, members are expected to perform certain functions and tasks, and they expect similar or complementary performances from others. Furthermore, groups exist within an organizational climate, and that climate is in large part the creation of the behavior of groups farther up in the hierarchy. These built-in conditions and reciprocal role expectations serve in some degree to keep things as they are and, as such, they constrain the ability of lower echelons to change until the change of upper echelons has created greater latitude for those below. In addition, by their own behavior and practices, upper managers indicate to lower managers what it is they really value and reward in the organizational system. Members of an organization are not likely to undertake change in any serious way if the practices implicit in the program deviate substantially from those of the head of the organization.

A constructive change effort has greater chance of success, therefore, where the president and other top officers start to apply the appropriate principles to their own operations before expecting any great extension of change throughout the lower echelons.

Constructive Change as a Rational Process

Constructive change is measurement centered; it begins with a quantitative reading of present location and direction of movement. Even more than this, it is throughout a rational process, making use of information, pilot demonstrations, and the persuasive power of evidence and hard fact.

A successful change effort begins with rigorous measurement of the way in which the organization is presently functioning. These measurements provide the material for a diagnosis which forms the basis for the design of a program of change activities. Likert has stated this quite pointedly in an early publication:

> One approach that can be used to apply the findings of human relations research to your own operation can be described briefly. Your medical departments did not order all of your supervisors nor all of your employees to take penicillin when it became available even though it is a very effective antibiotic. They have, however, administered it to many of your employees. But note the process of deciding when it should be administered. The individual was given certain tests and measurements obtained: temperature, blood analyses, etc. The results of these measurements were compared with known facts about diseases, infections, etc. and the penicillin was prescribed when the condition was one that was known or believed to be one that would respond to this antibiotic.
>
> We believe the same approach should be used in dealing with the human problems of any organization. This

suggests that human relations supervisory training programs should not automatically be prescribed for all
supervisory and management personnel. Nor should
other good remedies or methods for improvement be applied on a blanket basis to an entire organization hoping
it will yield improved results.[8]

One of the reasons for the importance of the diagnostic
step early in the life of a change program is explicitly stated
in the preceding quotation: it will increase the probability of
focusing upon the right, not the wrong, problems, and it will
add to the likelihood of the right, not the wrong, course of
treatment being prescribed. A clear statement of the problems, courses of action, and change objectives, based upon
sound measurements allied to the best possible conceptualization from research and theory will maximize the likelihood
that true causal conditions, rather than mere symptoms, will
be dealt with.

Another reason why sound diagnostic measurement is
important has to do with the motivating property of perceptual discrepancies to most human beings. For example, if a
person makes what he intends to be a witty remark at a cock-
tail party, and receives frowns, and stony silence instead of
laughter, he moves rapidly to alleviate the situation (if he
can). A discrepancy between the strength which a political
candidate has assumed he enjoys among his constituents and
a reading from a reliable poll often causes him to shift his
campaign strategy. In the same way, measurements which
point out previously unrecognized differences between what
really is going on in an organization and what is desired or intended by its managers have a motivating effect toward
change. Complacency gives way in some measure to a sense
of urgency for improvement where the direction of the discrepancy reveals probable shortcomings. Needless to say, the
organization's managers, when confronted with a discrepancy

of this type, must believe that change is possible and that the measurements are reliable, valid indicators of the organization's functioning. If not, they will probably reject the measurements and move away from, not toward, change.

In addition to a diagnosis as a starting point, a successful change program requires that a substantial amount of developmental research be conducted before embarking upon a full-scale application. The specific pattern of relationships among persons and groups, the size, direction, and time lag of connections among behaviors and events at various locations in the organization, and the specific usefulness in this instance of particular activities or treatments must be both known and proved to the satisfaction of organizational members. Although in small organizations this may perhaps be done with the whole organization as the focus of attention, in large corporations it may be essential to conduct a small pilot project to eliminate the usual difficulties prior to a large-scale application. Such a pilot project will enable a large firm to develop and test a change operation on a small and manageable scale, much as it pilot tests new technical processes. Because developmental research and pilot projects carry some risk of the occurrence of mistakes, it is perhaps wisest to locate these activities in a relatively small operation, preferably one that is self-contained. In a small unit, all participants will be more likely to be aware that an experiment is under way, as well as to know its general character and purpose. When mistakes do occur, they can be caught promptly and information about them shared with all relevant participants.

A pilot project's chances for success are increased if it is staffed by those persons whose present managerial style is closest to the principles and practices called for by System 4. As it progresses, it can then become a valuable training resource, a living example through which other promising managers can be rotated to gain experience and skill.

There is, therefore, in Likert's writings pertaining to organizational change a strong emphasis upon the role of information, objectivity, and rationality. Values and expectations, growing as they do from experience, are more symptom than cause of organizational difficulty. Ignorance and skepticism are the more immediate hurdles and, although the process by which fact is introduced is important and not all skeptics will be persuaded by such sound evidence as can be assembled, change is not likely to occur through an approach which ignores information input.

Constructive Change as a Participative Process

Too often, those involved in development and training work force a choice between accurate analytic information and participative process. For some, the participative character of group process is the all-important thing; accuracy and comprehensiveness of information that forms the group's basis for action is distinctly secondary in importance. For those of this persuasion, collecting and analyzing information about the organization's current state in relation to what is known about organizations generally becomes a didactic exercise, more important for the participation it stimulates than for its accuracy or for the rightness of the conclusions which come from it.

For others, precisely the reverse occurs. Information accuracy and the soundness of conclusions become all-encompassing, and a rather rapid drift often occurs to a form of directive lecturing. Good participative process and the involvement and motivation which it generates are sacrificed in favor of correctness.

It would appear to be Likert's view that, for constructive change to occur, neither can safely be ignored. It is important that quantitative information, carefully collected and analyzed, be brought to bear upon the problems facing the organization. It is equally important that this information be digested and applied in the course of a process which is participative. It is precisely the responsibility of those concerned with managing change to find the external and internal resource persons who, when combined, can provide both accurate information inputs and a participative process capable of integrating those inputs with wishes, feelings, and needs of members into a course of action to which all can give genuine commitment. It is not a choice of one or the other; it is a task of finding that way which guarantees both.

In this context, outside resource persons are likely to be more objective than those inside the organization, both because external individuals are likely to be better able to resist pressures against objectivity and because inside persons are often so close to the problems that they confuse symptoms and causes. On the other hand, those inside the organization know more about that specific organization; under conditions of trust and low pressure, they are likely to obtain better cooperation in implementing change activities. The collaboration of the two has a greater likelihood of resulting in an accurate reading, a reasonable plan for application, and commitment to the course of action decided upon. Likert discusses this in the following terms:

> It is common experience that orders by themselves are seldom sufficient to produce effective change in an organization and its functioning. Other procedures including those which make some use of participation usually are required. The persons who need to seek the participation or cooperation of the others are those persons who possess information as to what changes might bring improvement. When this information is based on research, it is the researchers, consequently, who are primarily faced with the problem of securing the participation and cooperation of the others if the research results are to be applied successfully. Moreover, applying new

ideas requires not only a knowledge of the new idea but also a full understanding of the present operation. The research staff, consequently, faces the problem of securing participation not only to facilitate cooperation in bringing about desirable changes, but also to be sure that the changes sought represent the best thinking based upon both past experience and current research findings.[9]

It is therefore in the wedding of the diagnostician's skills with the catalyst of participative group process that constructive change begins. The presentation of sound information within a meaningful theoretical framework will, particularly if it shows some moderate discrepancy from the assumed state of affairs, be a motivational force for change for a reasonably participative group. A blatant laying on of startling findings, together with what may be naive recommendations, will not. Also, those concerned solely with the "here and now" of group process will solve few organizational problems and produce little change within the confines of that process since much of what they must deal with is neither here nor now. To summarize, constructive change is a gradual process of successive increments, both because lag time causes it to be so and because movement cannot at any point exceed the currently legitimate boundaries of participants and succeed. It occurs by cooperation, not by hostile confrontation, and proceeds from the top of the organization down. It is rational, makes use of sound measurement, experimentation, analysis, and research as new inputs to a participative process which arrives at objectives for improvement. Neither information accuracy nor participative process can safely be sacrificed. For the person who proposes to design and guide an effort at organizational change, these principles point to a difficult and challenging role. He must be objective and analytic, know exactly what is wrong and what is right in the system's current functioning, how this relates to the more general body of knowledge about organizations, and what possibilities exist for constructive action. He must know all of this, and he must feel that it is incumbent upon him to gain the organization's acceptance of it. Still, he must abide by participative rules himself, helping the group to generate from its own acceptance of reality and its own understanding an action plan to which group members are prepared to commit themselves. It is easy to lecture or preach on the basis of research findings; it is also easy to immerse others in a cathartic process of "now-we-laugh-now-we-cry" emotion which leaves them sedated but not really better off. Constructive change, however, is more difficult.

CHAPTER 11

Questions and Answers

It is customary to conclude a book of principles and ideas with a summary chapter which either states in a few words what has already been said or orients the reader to what remains for others to say and do in the future. Neither alternative carried great appeal to this writer, the first because it inclines toward a dull recitation of what is already considerably simplified, the second because it seems somewhat impertinent.

It seems more appropriate that this book conclude with a series of questions posed to Rensis Likert himself. The questions selected are those which suggest themselves as most likely to occur to readers in the form of "certainly he does not mean . . . " or "but what about . . . ?"

Accordingly, the following questions have been posed:

1. If we build effective groups, knowing that group experience shifts values and beliefs over time, are we not being manipulative?
2. Is behavior by the supervisor which emphasizes high performance goals really consistent with a participative stance?
3. Much has been made in the preceding chapters about the importance of what might be termed the "cognitive" aspects of organizational behavior, e.g., the importance of measurement, of understanding principles and concepts of management, and ultimately of developing a system of human resources accounting. Some other writers and many practitioners currently emphasize the emotional aspects as more fundamental, that it is through the interplay of strong feelings, through confrontation with oneself and with others that organizationally meaningful events occur. How do you view this discrepancy?
4. What is likely to occur to union-management relationships when a company shifts to System 4?
5. Are participative groups universally useful to the management process, that is, are they really appropriate to top executive echelons, for example?

Dr. Likert's answers to these questions, provided to this writer, are presented in the remainder of this final chapter. A brief rephrasing of each question is presented immediately ahead of his response.

Question 1:   *Are effective groups manipulative?*

Dr. Likert: If the only direction of influence in effective groups were from the group to the individual and if in System 4 organizations the only direction of influence was from the top of the organization downward, then no doubt building an organization of effective groups could be viewed as manipulative. In fact, however, neither of these conditions exists. Members of a group are influenced by it, but each is capable also of exerting influence; as recent studies by Moscovici, Faucheux, Lage, and Naffrechoux show, an individual member of a group can exert great influence on the rest of the members.

The interaction processes in System 4 organizations, moreover, differ from those in Systems 1, 2, and 3 in enabling individual members to exert substantially more upward influence. This is true for all hierarchical levels but it is especially true for the lowest. So long as an organization adheres to System 4 processes and makes effective use of group problem solving, there is little or no danger that the groups of which it is composed will have manipulative impact on their members.

Question 2: *Is the supervisor's emphasis upon high performance goals consistent with participation?*

Dr. Likert: I believe the discussion under "High Performance Aspirations" on pages 51–52 of *The Human Organization* answers this question.

The third concept whose influence on organizational effectiveness will be considered deals with performance goals. Many studies [Kahn, 1958; Miller & Form, 1964] show that employees rather generally want stable employment, job security, opportunities for promotion, and satisfactory compensation. They also wish to be proud of the company they work for and of its performance and accomplishments. Since these needs and desires are important to the members of the organization, the principle of supportive relationship requires that they be met. This can be done best by an organization which is economically successful. A firm must succeed and grow to provide its employees with what they want from a job: pride in the job and company, job security, adequate pay, and opportunities for promotion. Economic success is a "situational requirement" [Likert, 1961, pp. 112, 211–20] which can be met only when the organization, its departments, and its members have high performance goals.

Superiors in System 4 organizations, consequently, should have high performance aspirations, but this is not enough. Every *member* should have high performance aspirations as well. Since these high performance goals should not be imposed on employees, there must be a mechanism through which employees can help set the high-level goals which the satisfaction of their own needs requires.

System 4 provides such a mechanism through: (1) group decision making and (2) multiple, overlapping group structure. As a consequence, System 4 organizations set objectives which represent an optimum integration of the needs and desires of the members of the organization, the shareholders, customers, suppliers, and others who have an interest in the enterprise or are served by it. Since economic and status needs are important to the members of an enterprise, the goal-setting processes of System 4 necessarily lead to high performance goals for each unit and for the entire firm. Any time these high performance aspirations do not exist, there is a deficiency in the interaction processes of the organization and a failure to recognize the situational requirements.[1] Barrett shows that when participation is used, there is greater congruity between the individual's goals and the organization's objectives.[2]

Question 3:   *How do you view confrontation, as opposed to informational activities, in organizational life?*

Dr. Likert: The underlying issue which this question raises is whether in modern society human behavior is changed more readily and *permanently* by the threat and exercise of punitive power or by sympathetic supportive behavior. In my judgment, the evidence from research is unequivocally clear. Widely different kinds of studies all yield the same conclusion: fear, punishment, and punitive force are appreciably less effective in bringing about behavioral changes which endure and in establishing new learned behavior than is supportive treatment including rewards used supportively. The principle of supportive relationships is as applicable to changing behavior in an organization as it is to achieving organizational effectiveness.

Emotionally charged confrontation leads to win-lose interaction. Blake, Shepard, and Mouton have described the results of extensive research which shows that win-lose confrontation heightens conflicts, intensifies differences, distorts perceptions, and leads to strong resistance to changing behavior rather than eager willingness to do so. Skinner has shown that persons modify behavior and learn more rapidly when desired behavior is rewarded than when undesired behavior is punished. Rogers has found that psychotherapy more often leads to constructive changes in behavior when it is supportive and client-centered rather than punitive and superimposed. Research in organizations shows clearly that at every hierarchical level supportive behavior and the application of the principle of supportive relationships by the superior more often leads to highly motivated behavior to help the organization achieve its goals than does punitive behavior by the superior.

When supportive behavior is used rather than win-lose confrontation, the members of an organization have the capability of using fully and effectively all of the available objective evidence to guide their behavior. Their perceptual and cognitive processes are not blinded and distorted by the emotional forces of bitterness, hostility, and unfavorable attitudes as occurs when win-lose confrontation is used.

Warden and others have shown that a typical learning cycle involves the following steps: (1) awareness that present behavior is inadequate since it fails to achieve the individual's goals; (2) search for alternate, more effective ways of behaving; (3) trials of these alternate ways to discover whether any of them enables the individual to achieve his goals successfully; (4) if any of the alternate ways of behaving yield success, the individual continues to use it in place of his original behavior; if none proves successful, the individual repeats the search-testing cycle.

In the search phase of this learning cycle the likelihood of finding a highly effective alternative will be increased greatly if the individual's search behavior is guided by principles and concepts which extensive research has shown to be most effective. The learning cycle, consequently, is much more likely to yield a successful alternative when the individual makes full use of all available cognitive resources.

We need further research on the dynamics of organizational change to test fully the relative effectiveness of alternate strategies of organizational change and to learn more about aspects of the process. It is my expectation that such research will show that supportive behavior is appreciably more effective than punitive treatment and that an important aspect of this superiority is the capacity of supportive behavior to facilitate the efficient functioning of cognitive processes. This will enable the organization and its members to make the best use of all information available to them.

Question 4:   *What happens to union-management relations under System 4?*

Dr. Likert: There is a sizable body of research findings which indicate that a shift to System 4 by a firm will improve union-management relationships substantially in the eyes of both the firm and the union. This is true for all hierarchical levels of management and for all employees. It is true also for all hierarchical levels of the union including both local unions and the regional and national officers in the national or international union.

This relationship between the management system used and the quality of union-management relationships has been found, in many different studies, to exist in all kinds of industrial enterprises and for widely different unions such as those in the AFL-CIO, the United Auto Workers, and the Teamsters. Moreover, the employees both as employees and as union members are much more satisfied with both the company and the union when the management system is System 4 or well toward it.

The data in these studies reveal also that shifts in the management system of a firm toward System 4 improve union-management relationships and shifts toward System 1 lead to worsened relationships. The improvement or worsening in union-management relationships when a shift is made in the management system of a firm does not occur, of course, simultaneously with the shift in the management system used. For the reasons discussed in your chapter 8, there is a lag time between shifts in the management system of a firm and the quality of union-management relationships.

When a shift toward System 4 brings improvement in union-management relationships, it is reflected in all the usual interactions between a firm and the union. Differences continue, but a capacity is developed to solve these differences in ways which are mutually satisfactory to the company and to the union. Grievances are resolved promptly and fairly and there are fewer grievances to be dealt with since the grievance machinery is not being used as an alternate communication channel to express the bitterness and hostility felt by the employees and the union toward management. Wildcats and slowdowns are unnecessary since problems and difficulties are dealt with by management and the union promptly and equitably. Bargaining and the negotiation of new contracts similarly are handled successfully by means of skillful problem solving which yields creative solutions acceptable to both parties.

The relationship between the management system used and the quality of union-management relations exists also for differences among plants or departments within a large corporation. That is, when the management of a plant is toward System 4, the relationships between the plant's management and the local union are much better than when the plant's management is toward System 1. This pattern has been found to exist even for plants in the same labor market.

Within a plant and local bargaining unit, studies show that the closer the first and second level (from the bottom) supervisors are to System 4 rather than to System 1 in their management style, the better the union-management relationships are within that small operating unit. In one large plant, for example, the findings revealed that the more often a foreman involved workers in decisions affecting them, the more favorable were the attitudes of the workers toward the firm. In those same shops it was found also that the more often the shop steward involved workers in decisions concerning union matters, the more favorable were their attitudes toward the union. In those sections where *both* the foremen and the shop steward involved workers in decisions affecting them, the union-management relationships were found to be excellent. Both management and the executive committee of the union referred to such shops as "sweet shops." These shops had few grievances and settled those which arose promptly and in a way satisfactory to all parties. On the other hand, those shops in which neither foremen nor shop stewards involved the workers in decisions were referred to by both the firm and the union as "sick shops." They had a long list of unresolved grievances, there was constant bickering and fighting, work stoppages and slowdowns occurred frequently, and other similar evidence of poor union-management relationships were commonplace.

Other research has shown that workers want both their union to be strong and their company to be successful. They want an effective union to protect their interests. They want the company they work for to be successful so that they have a secure job in a firm which can pay them well. This means, of course, that workers want both their company and their union to use System 4.

Question 5:   *Are participative groups universally useful to the management process?*

Dr. Likert: There is a steadily increasing body of research findings which demonstrates that at *every* hierarchical level in an organization, System 4 participative groups enable the organization to accomplish its objectives more successfully than other forms of leadership and management. There is, of course, less evidence available concerning top management than the lowest echelons since in any one corporation, subsidiary, or decentralized division, there is only one top management group while there are many work groups at the lowest echelon. Nevertheless, the results being obtained in recent years for the top echelons of both total corporations and their relatively independent subsidiary units are yielding consistent evidence that top echelons perform better when they use the System 4 participative group model.

There is, however, a tremendous difference in the impact on corporate success between the use of the System 4 participative model by the top echelon and by lower echelons. The impact upon the success of an organization of excellent performance by a work group is far greater when the work group is at a high rather than a low level in the firm. As you point out in chapter 8, the organizational climate created by the behavior and decisions of the top echelon of a firm exerts great influence upon the behavior and performance of lower levels. Consequently, the System 4 participative model is not only appropriate for the top echelon, it is *essential* that the top echelon use it to provide the organizational climate required to encourage lower echelons to use System 4 management.

Notes

Chapter 1

1. Rensis Likert, *New Patterns of Management* (New York: McGraw-Hill, 1961).
2. Rensis Likert, *The Human Organization* (New York: McGraw-Hill, 1967).

Chapter 2

1. Rensis Likert, *New Patterns of Management* (New York: McGraw-Hill, 1961), p. 104.

Chapter 3

1. Rensis Likert, *New Patterns of Management* (New York: McGraw-Hill, 1961), p. 82.

2. Rensis Likert, "Developing Patterns of Management I," General Management Series, no. 178 (New York: American Management Association, 1955), p. 16.
3. Likert, *New Patterns of Management*, p. 112.
4. Ibid., pp. 108–9.
5. Ibid., p. 190.

Chapter 4

1. Rensis Likert, *New Patterns of Management* (New York: McGraw-Hill, 1961), p. 116.
2. J. W. Atkinson, "Motivational Determinants of Risk-Taking Behavior," *Psychological Review* 64 (1957): 359–72.

Chapter 5

1. Rensis Likert, *New Patterns of Management* (New York: McGraw-Hill, 1961), pp. 46–47.
2. Rensis Likert, *The Human Organization* (New York: McGraw-Hill, 1967), pp. 108–9.

Chapter 6

1. Rensis Likert, *New Patterns of Management* (New York: McGraw-Hill, 1961), pp. 186–87.
2. Rensis Likert, *The Human Organization* (New York: McGraw-Hill, 1967), p. 158.
3. Ibid., p. 161.

Chapter 7

1. Rensis Likert, *New Patterns of Management* (New York: McGraw-Hill, 1961), pp. 94–95.

2. Ibid., p. 103.
3. Rensis Likert, *The Human Organization* (New York: McGraw-Hill, 1967), pp. 60–61.
4. Likert, *New Patterns of Management*, p. 171.
5. Likert, *The Human Organization*, pp. 56–57.

Chapter 8

1. Rensis Likert and D. Bowers, "Improving the Accuracy of P/L Reports by Estimating the Change in Dollar Value of the Human Organization," *Michigan Business Review* 25, no. 2 (March, 1973):15–24.

Chapter 9

1. Rensis Likert, *New Patterns of Management* (New York: McGraw-Hill, 1961), pp. 72–73.
2. Rensis Likert, *The Human Organization* (New York: McGraw-Hill, 1967), p. 149.
3. Rensis Likert, "Motivational Approach to Management Development," *Harvard Business Review* 37, no. 4 (1959): 77.
4. Rensis Likert, "An Emerging Theory of Organization, Leadership and Management," in *Leadership and Interpersonal Behavior*, ed. L. Petrullo (New York: Holt, Rinehart and Winston, 1961), p. 72.
5. Rensis Likert, "Developing Patterns of Management I," *General Management Series*, no. 178 (New York: American Management Association, 1955), p. 12.
6. R. Brummet, E. Flamholtz, W. Pyle, eds., *Human Resource Accounting* (Ann Arbor, Mich.: Foundation for Research on Human Behavior, 1969).
7. Likert, *The Human Organization*, pp. 102–3.
8. Rensis Likert and S. Seashore, "Making Cost Control Work," *Harvard Business Review* 41 (1963):101.

Chapter 10

1. Rensis Likert, *New Patterns of Management* (New York: McGraw-Hill, 1961), p. 55.
2. Ibid.
3. Rensis Likert, *The Human Organization* (New York: McGraw-Hill, 1967).
4. Likert, *New Patterns of Management*, p. 242.
5. Rensis Likert, "Motivational Dimensions of Administration," *America's Manpower Crisis* (Chicago: Public Administration Service, 1952), p. 115.
6. Rensis Likert, "Findings of Research on Management and Leadership," *Proceedings of the Pacific Coast Gas Association* 43 (1952):32.
7. Likert, *New Patterns of Management*, p. 245.
8. Likert, "Findings of Research on Management and Leadership," p. 35.
9. Rensis Likert and R. Lippitt, "The Utilization of Social Science," in *Research Methods in the Behaviorial Sciences*, ed. L. Festinger and D. Katz (New York: Holt, Rinehart and Winston, 1965), p. 603.

Chapter 11

1. Rensis Likert, *The Human Organization* (New York: McGraw-Hill, 1967), pp. 51–52.
2. J. H. Barrett, *Individual Goals and Organizational Objectives* (Ann Arbor, Mich.: Institute for Social Research, 1970).

Bibliography

Atkinson, J. W. "Motivational Determinants of Risk-Taking Behavior." *Psychological Review* 64 (1957):359–72.

Barrett, J. H. *Individual Goals and Organizational Objectives.* Ann Arbor, Mich.: Institute for Social Research, 1970.

Brummet, R., Flamholtz, E., and Pyle, W., eds. *Human Resource Accounting.* Ann Arbor, Mich.: Foundation for Research on Human Behavior, 1969.

Likert, R. "What Psychology Can Contribute to Industrial Stability." *Mechanical Engineering*, April, 1934, pp. 203–6.

———. "Organizing for Effective Selling." *New Problems of Sales Management.* Marketing Series, no. 35. New York: American Management Association, 1939, pp. 19–26.

———. "Democracy in Agriculture–Why and How?" *Yearbook of Agriculture*, 1940, pp. 994–1002.

——. "Findings of Research on Management and Leadership." *Proceedings of the Pacific Coast Gas Association* 43 (1952):28–35.

——. "Motivational Dimensions of Administration." *America's Manpower Crisis*. Chicago: Public Administration Service, 1952, pp. 89–117.

——. "Public Relations and the Social Sciences." *Public Relations Journal* 9, nos. 2 and 3 (1953):3–6, 11–15.

——. "Motivation: The Core of Management." Personnel Series, no. 155. New York: American Management Association, 1953, pp. 3–21.

——. "Developing Patterns of Management I." General Management Series, no. 178. New York: American Management Association, 1955, pp. 1–29.

——. "Developing Patterns of Management II." General Management Series, no. 182. New York: American Management Association, 1956, pp. 3–29.

——. "The Changing Role of the Company President." *Enterprise*, April 1957, pp. 37–38.

——. "Motivational Approach to Management Development." *Harvard Business Review* 37, no. 4 (1959):75–82.

——. "How to Raise Productivity 20%." *Nation's Business* 47, no. 8 (1959):30–32.

——. "An Emerging Theory of Management Applicable to Public Administration." In *Administrative Leadership in Government: Selected Papers*, ed. D. L. Bower and R. H. Pealy, pp. 1–15. Ann Arbor, Mich.: Institute of Public Administration, 1959.

——. "Influence and National Sovereignty." In *Festschrift for Gardner Murphy*, ed. J. G. Peatman and E. L. Hartley, pp. 214–27. New York: Harper, 1960.

——. "An Emerging Theory of Organization, Leadership and Management." In *Leadership and Interpersonal Behavior*, ed. L. Petrullo. New York: Holt, Rinehart and Winston, 1961.

——. *New Patterns of Management*. New York: McGraw-Hill, 1961.

———. "Supervision." *International Science and Technology*, no. 3 (1962):57–62.

———. "New Patterns in Sales Management." In *Changing Perspectives in Marketing Management*, ed. M. R. Warshaw, pp. 1–25. Ann Arbor, Mich.: University of Michigan, Bureau of Business Research, 1962.

———. "Improving Management through Continuing Research." *Personnel Administration* 26, no. 5 (1963): 5–11.

———. "Trends toward a World-wide Theory of Management." *Organizational Research and Theory—Its Implications for Management*. New York: CIOS XIII International Management Congress, 1963, pp. 110–14.

———. "The Use of Organizational Theory in Increasing Productivity in the Business Firm." In *Business Schools and Economic Growth*, ed. F. A. Bond, pp. 43–62, Michigan Business Papers, no. 39. Ann Arbor, Mich.: Bureau of Business Research, University of Michigan, 1964.

———. *The Human Organization*. New York: McGraw-Hill, 1967.

———. "Diagnose Your Teaching Role." *The Instructor*, Aug.–Sept., 1968, pp. 50–51.

———. "Introduction." In *Human Resource Accounting*, ed. R. Brummet, E. Flamholtz, and W. Pyle, pp. 1–10. Ann Arbor, Mich.: Foundation for Research on Human Behavior, 1969.

———. *The Relationship between Management Behavior and Social Structure*. Tokyo: CIOS XV International Management Congress, 1969.

Likert, R., and Bowers, D. "Organizational Theory and Human Resource Accounting." *American Psychologist* 24, no. 6 (1969):585–92.

———. "Improving the Accuracy of P/L Reports by Estimating the Change in Dollar Value of the Human Organization." *Michigan Business Review* 25, no. 2 (1973):15–24.

Likert, R., Bowers, D., Brummet, R., Norman, R., and Pyle, W. *Mobilizing Economic Forces to Accelerate Organiza-*

tional Development. Paper presented at the McGregor Conference, Massachusetts Institute of Technology, October, 1967.

Likert, R., Bowers, D., and Norman, R. "How to Increase a Firm's Lead Time in Recognizing and Dealing with Problems of Managing Its Human Organization." *Michigan Business Review* 21, no. 1 (1969):12–17.

Likert, R., and Lippitt, R. "The Utilization of Social Science." In *Research Methods in the Behavioral Sciences*, ed. L. Festinger and D. Katz. New York: Holt, Rinehart and Winston, 1965.

Likert, R., and Seashore, S. "Making Cost Control Work." *Harvard Business Review* 41 (1963):96–108.

Index